D0210486

RICHARD J. FOSTER'S
STUDY GUIDE FOR
CELEBRATION OF DISCIPLINE

RICHARD J. FOSTER'S STUDY GUIDE FOR CELEBRATION OF DISCIPLINE

Richard J. Foster

HarperSanFrancisco

An Imprint of HarperCollins*Publishers*

A STUDY GUIDE TO CELEBRATION OF DISCIPLINE. Copyright © 1983 by Richard J. Foster. All rights reserved. Printed in the United States of America. No part of this book may be used or reproduced in any manner whatsoever without written permission except in the case of brief quotations embodied in critical articles and reviews. For information address HarperCollins Publishers, 10 East 53rd Street, New York, NY 10022.

HarperCollins Web Site: http://www.harpercollins.com
HarperCollins®, 🏢 ®, and HarperSanFrancisco™ are trademarks of HarperCollins Publishers Inc.

04 05 RRD   50 49 48 47 46

To Ken and Doris Boyce
who believed in me and encouraged me
and filled a great void within me when the lives of
my own parents were cut short

CONTENTS

ACKNOWLEDGMENTS

Debts of friendship and help are unrepayable, but one can at least acknowledge the debt. The support and encouragement of my wife, Carolynn, and our boys, Joel and Nathan, have been superb, especially when the "writing marathon" began.

This Study Guide would not have been written were it not for the efficiency and support of my administrative assistant, Karen Christensen. At one point in the project I stood in my office glaring at my crowded datebook and declared, "It can't be done!" Quietly, Karen responded, "But it *can* be done," and so it was.

Many others helped bring the Study Guide into its present form. My special thanks go to Lee Farley Burkhart for her persistent concern that a study guide be produced for the many small groups studying *Celebration of Discipline*. Several of the study questions in the present volume owe their inspiration to her. Thanks, too, to Dorothy Craven and David Holly, who read the manuscript and offered many helpful comments. My greatest debt, however, is to the untold number of individuals who, through letters, in the classroom, and in seminars throughout the country, have helped to shape and sharpen my own understanding of (and experience in) the Spiritual Disciplines.

PREFACE

If I rightly understand the concept of a study guide, it has two purposes. First, a study guide is designed to highlight the issues raised in the book. Second, it is designed to enlarge and to further the discussion of the book. These two goals are virtual opposites. One tries to nail things down; the other tries to open things up. One tries to narrow the discussion; the other tries to broaden the discussion. But both are essential in any genuine learning situation.

The brief essays that begin each chapter are usually aimed at broadening and illuminating the landscape of the Discipline. This is especially true with the introductory chapter, in which I attempt to expose to your view the foundation upon which the Spiritual Disciplines are built. In a couple of the essays, I do try to clarify several items mentioned in the book.

Each essay is followed by a list of Scripture passages for personal or group study. It is of utmost importance that we flesh out our understanding of the Spiritual Disciplines in light of the Bible, for it is our sure foundation in all matters of faith and practice.

It is important that you understand the function of the study questions. While some of the questions are aimed at helping you to read the book carefully (that is, they fulfill the first goal of making the issues clear), most of the questions are meant to encourage an expanded understanding of the Spiritual Disciplines. The questions do not have answers that are a foregone conclusion. They are not intended to elicit parrot-like responses; instead they are meant to encourage thought and discussion. In compiling the questions, I have kept in mind the perceptive comment of John Ciardi: "A good question is never answered. It is not a bolt to be tightened into place but a seed to be planted and to bear more seed toward the hope of greening the landscape of ideas."

Obviously, the bibliographies are provided in the hope that you will become drawn into the subject and desire further exploration. The books provide markings for your journey. I have attempted to include a healthy variety, from literature for the beginner to more advanced reading. Hopefully, the annotations will guide you to select those books that meet your specific needs. For each chapter I have included several of the recognized classics in the field.

It is my hope that this study guide will serve in some small way to enhance your ability to be attentive to the voice of the true Shepherd. If these words (which are a broken and fragmentary witness at best) can direct you to Jesus Christ, your ever-living, ever-present Teacher, they will have served their purpose.

RICHARD J. FOSTER

March 1982
Friends University

INTRODUCTION: THE GOOD LIFE

It is one thing to praise discipline, and another to submit to it.—Don Quixote de La Mancha

If we expect to enter wholeheartedly into the experience of the Spiritual Disciplines, we must understand clearly that these Disciplines open us to the Good Life.* Their purpose is not to make life miserable but joyful, not to put us in bondage but to set us free, not to confine but to liberate.

There is a general cultural confusion today about the Good Life. And given the popular notion of abundance, it is almost impossible to believe that God is good and that His desire is to fill our lives with His goodness. In the modern world, the Good Life is often identified with power, wealth, status, and freedom from all authority. We have today two systems of teaching about the abundant life that are diametrically opposed to one another. One system has its roots in the culture around us; the other has its roots in the God of Abraham, Isaac, and Jacob. Both claim to bring us into the Good Life, and we must underscore the fact that their teachings are mutually exclusive.

We will never see the classical Disciplines of the spiritual life as a good thing until we perceive their function of bringing us into the abundant life of the Kingdom of God. And we cannot see this until we are able to understand how life under God and in His Kingdom is truly good and ultimately fulfilling, as opposed to the "good life" of human invention.

---

*It was my friend Dr. Dallas Willard, Associate Professor of Philosophy at the University of Southern California, who first helped me to see the connection between the Spiritual Disciplines and the classical discussions of the Good Life. I owe a great debt to him in helping me to understand what makes life abundant through both his teaching and his life.

1

In the Bible, we see that God desires to give each of us a full life and that abundance consists in the proper correlation of at least three things: provision, place, and personality. Human life is such that goodness consists in a combination of these three.

Provision

Provision means all things necessary to carry on human life adequately. God intends that we should have enough to care for ourselves. In human society, there is misery from a simple lack of provision—witness the immense suffering of many in the Third World. Christianity is the most materialistic of the world's religions: that is, it takes material things seriously as created goods God has given us to enjoy.

The Old Testament contains promise after promise of provision. "The Lord your God will bless you in all you produce and in all the work of your hands, so that you will be altogether joyful" (Deut. 16:15). Note that the rejoicing is because of the abundant provision from the hand of God. The New Testament picks up this same theme of God's care for those who trust in Him. Jesus makes it unmistakably clear that all those who seek first His Kingdom and His righteousness have all of the provision necessary for a happy life. We will be more adequately cared for than the lilies of the field.

On the other hand, we must beware of how people have taken the teaching on provision and twisted it into a thing of their own. It has been turned into a religion of personal peace and prosperity, crudely stated, "Love Jesus and get rich." However, it is also incarnated in much more subtle but equally destructive forms. And the interesting things about all these gimmicks to get blessedness is that they work; that is, they work if what we want is a little money. But if we desire the abundant life of the Kingdom of God—a life filled with holiness and free of avarice—they fail miserably.

What we need to see is that provision is a limited good, limited in the sense that we cannot make a life out of it. The moment we make a life out of provision, we deify it and lose the spiritual grace of contentment. We must never deny the fact that provision is good, but we must always understand that it is a limited good.

I should add that under the concept of provision is the importance of the adequate provision of time. People whose lives are fractured

2

and fragmented cannot know abundance. We all need adequate time for reflection, meditation, rest, conversation. The reasons many of us do not have the timeful life are varied, but the root problem is one of failing to live in the Christian grace of simplicity. It is easy to see that the Spiritual Disciplines of meditation, solitude, and simplicity deal in large part with the concept of provision.

Place

Place is the second element essential to the Good Life. Place is a *mutually understood* and *accepted* set of personal relationships that give identity to one's life. When I say that place must be "mutually understood," I mean that everyone involved needs to have the same expectation level of an individual's place. When I use the word "accepted," I mean that place should be viewed as a good thing. (It is very common today to view place as bad.)

Obviously, place is more a social function than a location. When we speak of refugees as "displaced persons," we are referring to more than the fact that they have had to leave their homes. We mean that all their roots have been torn up and their whole sense of identity as persons has been shattered.

Scripture has a great deal to say about place. In the Old Testament world, there was a place for the aged, the widowed, the orphaned. Today there is no real place for these people in the mainstream of human society. (The church today is struggling to find place for the divorced, and that single struggle accounts for an immense amount of grief in contemporary society.)

The New Testament describes the church as a set of places. The Apostle Paul is describing the places of the various members of the body of Christ when he discusses the spiritual gifts. There is a place, a proper function, for the apostle, the prophet, the evangelist, the teaching pastor, and all the gifts of the Spirit. The Epistles include quite sensitive and sensible descriptions of the place of the husband and wife, the parent and child, the slave and master. In our day, some people have horribly misunderstood these instructions and have used them to manipulate and to control other human beings. Others, deeply fearful of the stereotypes that have been given to place, have rejected the concept of place altogether. Neither group has understood the teaching of Scripture; both end in misery.

3

We must understand that there is simply no abundant life apart from place. That statement goes down hard today, especially among people who have felt oppressed by their place (and we should reject oppressive places), but we cannot be placeless. As long as we are finite, we must have a sense of place, a role, a function.

You can quickly see that the Spiritual Disciplines of submission, service, and guidance deal with the question of place.

Personality

The third element that needs to be integrated into human life for there to be abundance could be called personality. Personality refers to the inward person, expressed in certain determinate ways or ingrained habits. This is a major problem for many of us. We have acquired habits that defeat us over and over again. It is at the level of habit that the main work of redemption occurs so far as the transformation of our lives is concerned. If we are going to experience the Good Life, certain deeply imbedded habits are required. Conversely, there are also certain ingrained habits from which we need to be liberated. Since our slavery occurs mainly at the habit level, our freedom is discovered primarily at this level. In short, I am speaking of power, power from God that enters the life and transforms the habit patterns.

Jesus diagnosed the Apostle Peter's problem this way: "The spirit is willing, but the flesh is weak." His statement graphically depicts the situation for many of us—though we want to do what is right, we seem unable. But Jesus Christ did not intend that problem to continue for Peter, nor does He intend it should continue for us. In Scripture, we are instructed on how the flesh can be brought into a working harmony with the spirit in obedience to the ways of God and in the context of contemporary life.

But this reality is not found in a few easy steps to blessedness. Rather, it involves a voluntarily accepted and consciously chosen course of action that includes both individual and group life which will set us before God in such a way that He can produce the needed change. The major task of *Celebration of Discipline* is to describe this process and to show how the personality can be transformed by the power of the Holy Spirit. It is a practical manual on sanctification.

4

The Failure of Law and Ritual

All of us are aware of the fact that we fall short of this grand vision of God's goodness for our lives. In a frantic scramble to experience adequate provision, we succumb to the golden calf of materialism. Then, in an attempt to exorcise the consumer demon, we cut back in such a way that we threaten the family's livability and the children's hopes for college education. Or, we become determined to understand who we are—to discover our sense of identity, our sense of place—but in the process develop inner habit patterns of egoism and downright arrogance. Or, perhaps, we begin to see victory over the ingrained habit of gluttony only to discover an inner pattern of anger that now comes bubbling to the surface. And the moment we think we are holding everything in line, the deep-seated patterns of pride cloud the entire landscape.

Human sin is written across the face of humanity. It is very real to us all and only serves to show our inability to enter the Good Life of the Kingdom of God.

From the beginning, men and women have sought to free themselves from this crushing human predicament. The normal means for solving our dilemma has been law and ritual. Either we set up a series of laws, which we hope will cover every situation, or we devise religious rituals. (It matters little which we use—high-church types usually tend toward ritual, low-church types toward law—they are in reality two sides to the same coin.) Neither law nor ritual succeeds in transforming the human personality, although, as Jesus mentioned, both often make quite nice-looking whitened sepulchres. A heavy exertion of the will may be employed to accomplish our goal, but the effort is doomed to failure. Paul Tournier writes, "To depend on one's own will-power, one's good resolutions, especially against the impulsions of instinct and the determinism of powerful, psychological complexes, is to ask for failure and for a perpetual conflict which will destroy rather than strengthen the forces of the person."

There is a proper place for the will, but it is not in transforming the inner person. The will functions in the *decision* to place our lives before God so that He may work within us, as the old spiritual puts it, "I have decided to follow Jesus." And that decision is a continual

5

one, for the following of Jesus is continual. The will plays an important part in the function of the Spiritual Disciplines, but we are never made righteous by exertion of the will. Righteousness is a gift from God, which comes as we place ourselves before Him.

The function of the Spiritual Disciplines is now clear. They are the *means* for receiving God's grace. God's desire is to bring us into that way of living in which our needs are cared for, our sense of identity as individuals is clarified, and the inward life becomes whole and unified. To this end, Jesus Christ lived, died, was resurrected, and ever lives to be our present prophet, priest, and king. The salvation that is in Christ involves not only the forgiveness of sins and heaven when we die, but the breaking of the power of sin so that we can live in newness of life now.

The Good Life of the Kingdom of God breaks into our hearts by the grace of God alone. We are not only saved by grace, but we live by it as well. However, we must see (and this is essential if we are to avoid the ancient heresy of antinomianism) that we have a part to play in the drama of holiness. To be sure, it is only a bit part in a huge pageant, but it is an essential one. Our work—our only work—is to place ourselves in the way of Christ and invite Him to work in our lives, individually and collectively. The Spiritual Disciplines are merely an attempt to describe how we can accomplish that work. They sketch out (surely, only in part) the means of grace whereby we are placed before God. Having done this, the Disciplines can do no more for us. Beyond this point, no human being can go. The change then is God's work, and as it comes, we sing joyfully, "Amazing grace, how sweet the sound, that saved a wretch like me."

Daily Scripture Readings

What modern thinkers call "the Good Life," biblical writers would identify as "the Godly Life." Our understanding is immeasurably deepened by studying scriptural examples of those who came to walk in the joy of the Lord.

Sunday: Jesus Christ: the *Summum bonum* of the Good Life / all four gospels beginning with Mark.

6

Monday: The example of Abraham / Genesis 12–25.

Tuesday: The example of Elijah / 1 Kings 17–19, 2 Kings 1–2.

Wednesday: The example of David / 1 Samuel 16–27, 2 Samuel 1–12, 22–23:7.

Thursday: The example of Daniel / Daniel 1–12.

Friday: The example of Peter / the gospels, Acts 1–5, Acts 10–11 (see also his epistles).

Saturday: The example of Paul / Acts 9, Acts 11–28 (see also his epistles).

Suggested Books for Further Study

There is nothing that gives content to the Good Life and fleshes out the meaning of our own spirituality quite like reading the saints throughout the ages. They lift our spirits, free us from the cult of the contemprary, and give us models to imitate.

Anderson, Courtney. *To the Golden Shore: The Life of Adoniram Judson.* Grand Rapids, Mich. Zondervan Publishing Co., 1977. (The moving story of the man who, through great suffering, burned the gospel into the heart of Burma.)

Brainerd, David. *The Life and Diary of David Brainerd.* Edited by Jonathan Edwards. Chicago: Moody Press, 1980. (In this fine book, Edwards reconstructs the inward conflicts and struggles of the soul of a godly pioneer missionary to the North American Indians.)

Brother Ugolino de Monte Sants. *The Little Flowers of St. Francis.* Translated by Raphael Brown. Garden City, N.Y.: Image Books, 1958. (Stories of early Franciscans that will delight, shock, and challenge you.)

The Confessions of Saint Augustine. Translated by Edward B. Pusey, D.D. New York: Collier Books, 1961. (The intense spiritual search of a man destined to become one of the major figures in Christian history.)

Fitts, A. P. *The Life of D. L. Moody.* Chicago: Moody Press, 1979. (The story of the evangelist who dared to see what God would do with a man totally committed to Him.)

Fox, George. *The Journal of George Fox.* Edited by John Nickalls. New York: Cambridge University Press, 1952. (The first of the modern journals and one that set the standard for the many that would follow, including the more famous *Journal of John Wesley.* Written by the major figure of seventeenth-century Quakerism, it is filled with power and vigor.)

Grubb, Norman. *Rees Howells Intercessor.* Ft. Washington, Penn.: Christian Literature Crusade, 1979. (The story of the Welshman who made prayer the most notable feature of his life.)

Journals of Jim Elliott. Edited by Elizabeth Elliott. Old Tappan, N.J.: Fleming H. Revell, 1978. (The powerful journal writings of one of the five men martyred by the Auca Indians at the middle of this century.)

Julian of Norwich. *Showings.* Translated by Edmund Colledge, O.S.A., and James Walsh, S.J. New York: Paulist Press, 1978. (Sixteen "Showings" or revelations of God's love, which came to Julian in a series of visions. A fourteenth-century English mystic, Julian and her revelations of the feminine side of God are of particular interest today.)

Madame Guyon. *Madame Guyon: An Autobiography.* Chicago: Moody Press, n.d. (This well-known seventeenth-century mystic wrote this introspective account of her life while in prison for her faith.)

Merton, Thomas. *The Seven Storey Mountain.* New York: Harcourt Brace, 1948. (The early days of the twentieth century's most famous Trappist monk. You might also want to read Monica Furlong's excellent *Merton: A Biography*, published by Harper & Row, 1980.)

Müller, George. *Autobiography of George Müller.* Edited by H. Lincoln Wayland. Grand Rapids, Mich.: Baker Book House, 1981. (The story of the man who interpreted for us the meaning of faith through his large orphanages and other Christian work, which he financed and sustained through prayer alone.)

Pascal's Pensees. Translated by W. F. Trotter. New York: Collier Books, 1960. (Terse statements on life and death by the acclaimed scientist, inventor, psychologist, philosopher, and Christian apologist of seventeenth-century France.)

Sadhu Sundar Singh. *At the Master's Feet.* Translated by Rev. Arthur and Mrs. Parker. Old Tappan, N.J.: Revell Company,

1922. (Moving words on the life of faith by "the Saint Paul of India." You may also want to read the powerful story of Sundar's life, *Sadhu Sundar Singh*, written by Cyril J. Davey and published in 1980 by STL Books, P.O. Box 48, Bromley, Kent, England.)

Seaver, George. *David Livingstone: His Life and Letters.* New York: Harper and Brothers, 1957. (The moving story of Livingstone's pioneer work in Africa, both in evangelism and in efforts to abolish the slave trade.)

Sheen, Fulton J. *Treasure in Clay: The Autobiography of Fulton J. Sheen.* New York: Doubleday, 1980. (An intimate biography by the archbishop who became so well known to Americans through his radio broadcasts and, later, his television series.)

Taylor, Dr. and Mrs. Howard. *J. Hudson Taylor: A Biography.* Chicago: Moody Press, 1965. (The story of the man who opened inland China to the gospel and learned to walk in faith in exceptional ways.)

Walker, F. Deauville. *William Carey: Father of Modern Missions.* Chicago: Moody Press, 1980. (The life of the man who called the world to "expect great things from God! Attempt great things for God!")

Wesley, John. *The Journal of John Wesley.* Edited by Percy Livingstone Parker. Chicago: Moody Press, 1951. (The journal record of the man who boldly said, "The world is my parish," and who founded the Methodist movement.)

Woolman, John. *The Journal and Major Essays of John Woolman.* Edited by Phillips P. Moulton. New York: Oxford Press, 1971. (In terms of the issues it addresses—that is, racism, war and peace, faith in God, etc.—this is the most contemporary of all the journals, in my opinion.)

9

1. THE SPIRITUAL DISCIPLINES: DOOR TO LIBERATION

As you begin this study of the Christian Disciplines, advance warning may help you to avoid several pitfalls. Briefly, I shall list seven of these pitfalls—though, surely, there are more.

The first pitfall is the temptation to turn the Disciplines into law. There is nothing that can choke the heart and soul out of walking with God like legalism. The rigid person is not the disciplined person. Rigidity is the most certain sign that the Disciplines have gone to seed. The disciplined person can do what needs to be done when it needs to be done. The disciplined person can live in the appropriateness of the hour. The disciplined person can respond to the movings of divine grace like a floating balloon. Always remember that the Disciplines are perceptions into life, not regulations for controlling life.

The second pitfall is the failure to understand the social implications of the Disciplines. The Disciplines are not a set of pious exercises for the devout, but a trumpet call to obedient living in a sin-racked world. They call us to wage peace in a world obsessed with war, to plead for justice in a world plagued with inequity, to stand with the poor and the disinherited in a world full of individuals who have forgotten their neighbors.

A third pitfall is the tendency to view the Disciplines as virtuous in themselves. In and of themselves, the Disciplines have no virtue, possess no righteousness, contain no rectitude. It was this important truth that the Pharisees failed to see. The Disciplines place us before God; they do not give us "brownie points" with God.

A fourth pitfall, similar to the third, is the tendency to center on the Disciplines rather than on Christ. The Disciplines were de-

10

signed for the purpose of realizing a greater good. And that greater good is Christ Himself, who must always remain the focus of our attention and the end of our quest.

A fifth pitfall is the tendency to isolate and elevate one Discipline to the exclusion or neglect of the others. The Disciplines are like the fruit of the Spirit—they comprise a single reality. Sometimes we become intrigued with fasting, for example, and we begin to think of that single Discipline as comprising the whole picture. What is only one tree we see as the whole forest. This danger must be avoided at all costs. The Disciplines of the spiritual life are an organic unity, a single path.

The sixth pitfall is the tendency to think that the twelve Disciplines mentioned in *Celebration* somehow exhaust the means of God's grace. I have no exhaustive list of the Christian Disciplines, and as far as I know, none exists. For who can confine the Spirit of God? *Celebration* is merely one attempt to compile those acts of devotion that the writers of Scripture and the saints throughout the history of the church have said were important in experiential faith. But Christ is greater than any attempt to describe His workings with His children. He cannot be confined to any system, no matter how worthy.

The seventh pitfall is the most dangerous. It is the temptation to study the Disciplines without experiencing them. To discuss the Disciplines in the abstract, to argue and debate their nature or validity—these activities we can carry out in comparative safety. But to step out into experience threatens us at the core of our being. And yet there is no other way. Prayerfully, slowly, perhaps with many fears and questions, we need to move into this adventurous life of the Spirit.

Daily Scripture Readings

Sunday: The longing to go deeper / Psalm 42.

Monday: The slavery of ingrained habits / Psalm 51.

Tuesday: The slavery of ingrained habits / Romans 7:13–25.

Wednesday: The bankruptcy of outward righteousness / Philippians 3:1–16.

11

Thursday: Sin in the bodily members / Proverbs 6:16–19.

Friday: Sin in the bodily members / Romans 6:5–14.

Saturday: The victory of Spiritual Discipline / Ephesians 6:10–20.

Study Questions

1. I say that "superficiality is the curse of our age." If you tend to agree, list several indicators in American culture that illustrate this. If you tend to disagree, list several indicators in American society that support your conviction. What current influences might cause the Christian people of this century to be more superficial than Christian folk of other centuries?
2. I refer to the Disciplines discussed in this book as "classical." What reason do I give for using this description and do you agree or disagree? Why?
3. What is the purpose of the Spiritual Disciplines?
4. What primary requirement must you have to embark on this journey? What things would keep you from fulfilling this requirement?
5. Consider carefully Heini Arnold's statement, "We want to make it quite clear that we cannot free and purify our own heart by exerting our own will." How does Arnold's statement compare with your own experience?
6. I indicate that those who desire to explore the world of the Spiritual Disciplines are faced with two difficulties. What is the "practical difficulty" and how can it be seen in your own life? What is the "philosophical difficulty" and how can it be seen in your own life?
7. What do I mean by "disciplined grace"? What does the concept of "cheap grace" mean? With which of these two types of grace are you most familiar?
8. If you were walking along the narrow ledge of which I speak, which side would you fall off of most often? Explain how this can be seen in your own life.
9. As you read this book, consider what you feel are its most dangerous elements. That is, what concepts presented here might lead people away from God, rather than to God?

12

10. What ideas struck you most forcefully in this chapter? Were there statements you disagreed with, or were unable to identify with, or perhaps found difficult to understand?

Suggestions for Further Study

There is a wealth of literature on the Spiritual Disciplines, and the following list represents some of the best works in the general field of the spiritual life. It provides an excellent background and framework out of which to study the Christian Disciplines.

Arnold, Heini. *Freedom from Sinful Thoughts.* New York: Plough Publishing House, 1973. (An insightful little book on inner thought-life by a leader in the Hutterian Society of Brothers.)

Bonhoeffer, Dietrich. *The Cost of Discipleship.* New York: The MacMillan Company, 1963. (The book that gave us the term "cheap grace" and so forcefully called us to a more costly form of discipleship.)

Brother Lawrence. *The Practice of the Presence of God.* Mt. Vernon, N.Y.: Peter Pauper Press, 1963. (These simple letters and conversations by Nicholas Herman [Brother Lawrence] of France have inspired three centuries of Christians to life in more intimate communion with Christ.)

Day, Albert Edward. *Discipline and Discovery.* Nashville, Tenn.: The Upper Room, 1977. (A manual written especially for the "Disciplined Order of Christ" but containing practical wisdom for us all. This updated workbook edition keeps this fine work available to us.)

Fénelon, Francois. *Christian Perfection.* Minneapolis: Bethany Fellowship (Dimension Books), 1975. (Letters of spiritual counsel and direction on a multitude of practical matters by the French Archbishop who advised numerous individuals in the court of Louis XIV. Other recent editions of his writings include *The Royal Way of the Cross* and *Let Go.*)

Francis de Sales. *Introduction to the Devout Life.* Translated by John K. Ryan. New York: Harper & Row, 1950. (Much of this material is the result of counsel Francis gave to a single individual, Mme. Louise Charmoisy, in the early seventeenth century. This work covers a wide variety of spiritual matters for

13

those seeking to deepen their devotional life.)

Freer, Harold Wiley. *Christian Disciplines*. New York: Pageant Press, 1960. (Short meditations that evidence an unusual awareness of the Devotional Classics.)

Jean-Pierre de Caussade. *The Sacrament of the Present Moment*. San Francisco: Harper & Row, 1982. (Written by an eighteenth-century French Jesuit; it is sheer delight to read.)

Kelly, Thomas R. *A Testament of Devotion*. New York: Harper & Row, 1941. (I can count on one hand the twentieth-century classics of devotion—this is one of them.)

Kempis, Thomas à. *The Imitation of Christ*. Translated by E. M. Blaiklock. Nashville, Tenn.: Thomas Nelson Publishers, 1979. (A new translation by E. M. Blaiklock adds fresh vitality to this undisputed leader of the classics of Christian devotion.)

Law, William. *A Serious Call to a Devout and Holy Life*. Edited by Paul G. Stanwood. New York: Paulist Press, 1978. (An influential work on the Christian life by the person often called the greatest of the post-Reformation English mystics. Law was the leader of a small spiritual community and included among his disciples John and Charles Wesley.)

Nee, Watchman. *The Normal Christian Life*. Fort Washington, Penn.: Christian Literature Crusade, 1964. (An important statement on the Christian life which stands in counter distinction to so much of "normal Christianity.")

Nouwen, Henri J. M. *Making All Things New*. San Francisco: Harper & Row, 1981. (A small but powerful invitation to the spiritual life centering on the Disciplines of solitude and community.)

O'Connor, Elisabeth. *Journey Inward, Journey Outward*. New York: Harper & Row, 1968. (More than a continuation of the story begun in *Call to Commitment*, this work sets forth in life situations the twin disciplines of the inward journey of devotion and the outward journey of service.)

Peterson, Eugene H. *A Long Obedience in the Same Direction*. Downers Grove, Ill.: InterVarsity Press, 1980. (Through a study of the "Songs of Ascents" [Psalms 120–134], Eugene Peterson helps Christians wrestle with many of the classical Spiritual Disciplines.)

Sanford, Agnes. *The Healing Light*. St. Paul, Minn.: Macalester

14

Park Publishing Co., 1972. (The classic statement on the healing ministry to which Jesus calls the church and a book that has influenced my own pilgrimage immensely.)

Taylor, Richard Shelley. *The Disciplined Life*. Minneapolis: Beacon Hill Press, 1962. (A sharp, stacatto plea for disciplined living in an age of self-indulgence.)

Tozer, A. W. *The Pursuit of God*. Harrisburg, Pa.: Christian Publications, 1948. (A tender sensitive book filled with insight and a catholicity of outlook that is refreshing.)

Anthologies of Devotional Classics

An Anthology of Devotional Literature. Edited by Thomas S. Kepler. Grand Rapids, Mich.: Baker Book House, 1977. (Contains selections of many of the important Christian writers from Clement of Rome to Karl Barth.)

The Doubleday Devotional Classics. Edited by Glenn Hinson. 3 vols. New York: Doubleday, 1978. (Contains a wide variety of choice specimens from the vast treasury of Protestant spirituality.)

Living Selections from the Great Devotional Classics. Nashville, Tenn.: The Upper Room (various dates). (Twenty-nine booklets that are available as a set or individually. An excellent introduction to some of the best of the devotional writers.)

15

PART I

The Inward Disciplines

2. THE DISCIPLINE OF MEDITATION

The purpose of meditation is to enable us to hear God more clearly. Meditation is listening, sensing, heeding the life and light of Christ. This comes right to the heart of our faith. The life that pleases God is not a set of religious duties; it is listening to His voice and obeying His word. Meditation opens the door to this way of living. Jean-Pierre de Caussade wrote, "There remains one single duty. It is to keep one's gaze fixed on the master one has chosen and to be constantly listening so as to understand and hear and immediately obey his will."

Meditation is a more passive Discipline. It is characterized more by reflecting than by studying, more by listening than by thinking, more by releasing than by grabbing. In the Discipline of meditation we are not so much acting as we are opening ourselves to be acted upon. We invite the Holy Spirit to come and work within us—teaching, cleansing, comforting, rebuking. We also surround ourselves with the strong light of Christ to protect us from any influence not of God.

Since some have asked, I might just as well come clean and tell you that I have *no* interest at all, nor experience, in astro-travel or any of the other rather exotic forms of meditation. Perhaps that reflects my own prejudice, but such approaches, it seems to me, do not resonate well with the biblical witness. I find little ethical content or concern for moral transformation in these forms of meditation. I am much more interested in the kind of hearing that Abraham, Moses, and Elijah knew, which brought forth a radical obedience to the one true God.

In *Celebration*, I gave only a brief description of the meditation upon Scripture, assuming that people were quite familiar with this form of meditation. In this assumption I was wrong, and so I should

19

like here to provide a brief meditation upon John 6 as an example of one approach to the *meditatio Scripturarum*. It is my hope that this will encourage all of us to drink deeply and extensively at this, the most central and important form of Christian meditation.

The story is a familiar one—Jesus' feeding of the five thousand. Begin by imagining yourself as the child who gave his lunch. Or, perhaps, imagine that you are one of the child's parents. At any rate, try to place yourself in the actual scene. Following the counsel of Ignatius of Loyola, attempt to use all of your senses as you slowly read the passage. Try to see the story—the grass, the hills, the faces of the people. Try to hear the story—the sound of the water, the noise of the children, the voice of the Master. Try to feel the story—the texture of your clothing, the hardness of the ground, the coarseness of your hands. Finally, try to feel with your emotions—hesitancy at bringing your lunch, astonishment at the miracle of multiplied food, joy at the gracious provision of God. At first this approach may necessitate several readings of the text.

Then, in your imagination, watch the crowd leave and Jesus go up into the hills. You are left alone. You sit on a rock overlooking the water and re-experience the events of the day. You become quiet, and after a little while, Jesus returns and sits on a nearby rock. For a time, you are both silent, looking out over the water perhaps and enjoying one another's presence. After a bit, the Lord turns to you and asks this question, "What may I do for you?" Then you tell Him what is in your heart—your needs, your fears, your hopes. If weeping or other emotions come, do not hinder them.

When you have finished, you become quiet for a little while. Then you turn to the Lord and ask, "What may I do for you?" And you listen with the heart quietly, prayerfully. No instruction needs to come, for you are just glad to be in Christ's presence. If some words do come to you, you take them with utmost seriousness. More often than not, they will be some utterly practical instruction about seemingly trivial matters, for God wants us to live out our spirituality in the ordinary events of our days. And I have often found them to be wonderful words of life. What I have shared here is, of course, only an example—God will, I am sure, give you many other ways to enter into the life of Scripture.

Beyond this, may I make a plea for the memorization of Scrip-

20

ture?* Through memorization, the biblical witness becomes rooted deeply in the inner mind and begins to mold and adjust our world view almost without our realizing it. Then, too, as we submit ourselves to this small discipline, God is able to reach us through the word of Scripture at any given moment, even as we sleep. Memorization is a helpful means to enhance our meditation upon Scripture.

Daily Scripture Readings

Sunday: The glory of meditation / Exodus 24:15–18.

Monday: The friendship of meditation / Exodus 33:11.

Tuesday: The terror of meditation / Exodus 20:18–19.

Wednesday: The object of meditation / Psalm 1:1–3.

Thursday: The comfort of meditation / 1 Kings 19:9–18.

Friday: The insights of meditation / Acts 10:9–20.

Saturday: The ecstasy of meditation / 2 Corinthians 12:1–4.

Study Questions

1. What are some of your first reactions to the idea of meditation? What is your background experience in this area?
2. What is the basic difference between eastern meditation and Christian meditation?
3. What things make your life crowded? Do you think you have a desire to hear the Lord's voice in the midst of all the clutter?
4. Experience the following words of Frederick W. Faber for fifteen minutes. Record what you learn from the experience.

> Only to sit and think of God,
>   Oh what a joy it is!
> To think the thought, to breathe the Name
>   Earth has no higher bliss.

---

*Contrary to popular myth, memorization is quite easy once one catches onto the idea. The Navigators have published numerous aids that make the task even more possible.

5. What threatens you most about meditation?
6. Have you ever considered dreams as a means of hearing from God? Have you had any experience in this area?
7. List the five forms for meditation that I give. Ponder the fifth form and what it might mean today, given the contemporary political scene.
8. What is the value of thinking through the specifics of time, place, and position during the meditation experience?
9. What are the dangers in concentrating on time, place, and position in the meditation experience?
10. Do "palms down, palms up" today. Note anything you learn about yourself.

Suggested Books for Further Study

Brother Lawrence and Frank Laubach. *Practicing His Presence.* Edited by Gene Edwards. Goleta, Calif.: Christian Books, 1981. (A helpful bringing-together of selections from *Letters by a Modern Mystic* and *The Game with Minutes* by Laubach and a modern rewrite of Lawrence's famous *The Practice of the Presence of God.*)

Downing, Jim. *Meditation: The Bible Tells You How.* Colorado Springs, Colo.: NavPress, 1976. (A practical little book by a leader among the Navigators on the active side of meditation upon scripture.)

Kelsey, Morton T. *The Other Side of Silence.* New York: Paulist Press, 1976. (The most important single book on the theology and psychology behind the experience of Christian meditation.)

Merton, Thomas. *Contemplative Prayer.* Garden City, N.Y.: Image Books, 1971. (A powerful analysis of the central nature of contemplative prayer. A must book.)

Merton, Thomas. *Spiritual Direction and Meditation.* Collegeville, Minn.: The Liturgical Press, 1960. (Written mainly with the monastic life in mind, but filled with discernment and a practical wisdom that all can appreciate.)

Moffatt, Doris. *Christian Meditation: The Better Way.* New York: Christian Herald Books, 1979. (Simple, meaningful prayer techniques and specific meditations that will help the beginner move forward into Christian meditation.)

O'Connor, Elizabeth. *Search for Silence*. Waco, Tex.: Word Books, 1972. (Brings into focus the art of quietness and contemplation through meaningful exercises and a wealth of quotations from the devotional masters.)

Russell, Marjorie. *A Handbook of Christian Meditation*. Old Greenwich, Conn.: Devin-Adair Company, 1978. (A practical, easy-to-understand guide to the actual methods of meditation.)

Tilmann, Klemens. *The Practice of Meditation*. Ramsey, N.J.: Paulist Press, 1977. (A handbook on Christian meditation that draws on both Eastern and Western tradition. The last third of the book has numerous meditations upon Scripture.)

3. THE DISCIPLINE OF PRAYER

As I travel, I find several common misconceptions that defeat the work of prayer.

The first misconception is the notion that prayer mainly involves asking things from God. Answers to prayer are wonderful, but they are secondary to the main function of prayer, which is a growing, perpetual communion. To sink down into the light of Christ and become comfortable in that posture, to sing, "He walks with me and He talks with me" and know it as a radiant reality, to discover God in all of the moments of our days, and to be pleased rather than perturbed at the discovery—this is the stuff of prayer. It is out of this refreshing life of communion that answered prayer comes as a happy by-product.

The second misconception is the view that prayer must always be a struggle, "getting under the burden of prayer," as we say. I certainly would not want to deny those times of intensity and difficulty, but I have not found that such times are the most common experience. Nor would I want to minimize the sense of awe, and even terror, which we feel in the presence of the Sovereign of the universe. And yet, the most frequent experience during prayer is one of lightness, joy, comfort, serenity. Even laughter comes at times, though it is richer and less pretentious (should I say, more holy) than ordinary laughing. There is a feeling of companionship, though again it is of a different quality from the ordinary human variety. Perhaps it is that we are becoming friends with God.

A third misconception is the idea that we live in a closed universe, that everything is fixed. We think, "Since everything is set and God knows the end from the beginning, why pray?" The question is a good one. Perhaps you have had the frustrating experience of talking with an employer about some company policy being considered for adoption. Your employer may invite you to share your concerns and may seem to listen intently. Then later you discover that the decision had already been made long before you ever entered the room. Many folk feel that prayer is a similar situation. But if the Apostle Paul is right that "we are fellow workers with God" (1 Cor. 3:9), then ours is indeed an open universe. We are working with God to determine the outcome of things. It needs to be said reverently, but it does need to be said: we are co-creators with God in advancing His kingdom upon the earth.

A fourth misconception is the fear that our faith will crumble if our prayers are not answered the first time every time. As one person put it to me, "If God doesn't answer this prayer, it is all over; I will never be able to believe in prayer again." It is this fear that causes us to gravitate toward vague prayers—then if nothing happens, no one is the wiser. But suppose I walk into my office and turn on the light and nothing happens. Would I say, "I never believed in electricity anyway"? No, I would assume something is wrong, and I would set out to find out what it is: perhaps the bulb is burned out or the wiring connections are faulty. The same is true with prayer, and very often I have found the problem is indeed a faulty connection on our end.

A fifth misconception about prayer is the common teaching, "Pray once! Any more than that shows a lack of faith." Now I understand the good intentions of people who teach this way, but, very frankly, it flies in the face of a great deal of biblical experience and teaching, especially Jesus' parables on importunity. We are to keep at this work, mainly, I think, because we are the channel through which God's life and light flows into individuals or situations. And, incidentally, I have found prayer to be the most helpful of the Disciplines in freeing us from the monsters of the past because of the inner healing that comes through the hands of those who pray for us.

May I call you to the adventure of prayer? Nothing draws us closer to the heart of God.

Daily Scripture Readings

Sunday: The pattern of prayer / Matthew 6:5–15.

Monday: The prayer of worship / Psalm 103.

Tuesday: The prayer of repentance / Psalm 51.

Wednesday: The prayer of thanksgiving / Psalm 150.

Thursday: The prayer of guidance / Matthew 26:36–46.

Friday: The prayer of faith / James 5:13–18.

Saturday: The prayer of command / Mark 9:14–29.

Study Questions

1. Why do I say, "To pray is to change"? Have you ever experienced that in your own life?
2. How can we keep from being discouraged by the example of the "giants of the faith"?
3. What difference does it make in our praying if we believe that we live in an "open universe"? A "closed universe"?
4. Why.is it important to view prayer as a learning process?
5. Distinguish between the prayer of faith and the prayer of guidance.
6. Frank Laubach said, "I want to learn how to live so that to see someone is to pray for them." Experiment with that approach to life for one whole day and record what you learn from the experience.
7. What is your response to the idea of using the imagination in the work of prayer?
8. *Look* at someone today and imagine what they could be if they received a double portion of the light of Christ. By faith, give that portion to them and record what you learn from the experience.
9. What should we do when we don't feel like praying?
10. What experience have you had of the Thomas Kelly statement on page 40 of *Celebration*?

Suggested Books for Further Study

Bounds, E. M. *Power through Prayer*. Grand Rapids, Mich.: Zondervan Publishing House, 1979. (This stimulating call to the ministry of prayer was written primarily for preachers but provides plenty of challenge to all who dare to read it.)

Grou, Jean Nicholas. *How to Pray.* Translated by Joseph Dalby. Nashville, Tenn.: The Upper Room, 1973. (This book by a French Jesuit of the eighteenth century is, in the words of Evelyn Underhill, "one of the best short expositions of the essence of prayer which has ever been written.")

Hallesby, Ole. *Prayer.* Minneapolis, Minn.: Augsburg Press, 1975. (Written by one of Norway's leading devotional writers, this book is aimed at helping the average Christian develop a more meaningful life of prayer.)

Kimmel, Jo. *Steps to Prayer Power.* New York: Abingdon Press, 1972. (A brief, intently practical, and genuinely helpful guide to prayer.)

Laubach, Frank C. *Prayer: The Mightiest Force in the World.* Old Tappan, N.J.: Fleming H. Revell Co., 1959. (A book born out of the practice and zeal of one of the truly great missionaries of the twentieth century who was often called "the apostle of literacy.")

Leech, Kenneth. *True Prayer.* San Francisco: Harper & Row, 1980. (Henri Nouwen said it well: "*True Prayer* not only speaks about prayer, but it creates the space in the reader where prayer can grow and mature.")

Murray, Andrew. *With Christ in the School of Prayer.* Old Tappan, N.J.: Fleming H. Revell Co., 1970. (A grand classic that deals with the ministry of intercession by a great preacher and prayer of the last century.)

Nee, Watchman. *The Prayer Ministry of the Church.* Hollis, N.Y.; Christian Fellowship Publishers, 1973. (More likely than not, this book will disturb you and challenge many of your cherished ideas about prayer and, as a result, force you to think about and experience more deeply the work of prayer.)

Sanders, J. Oswald. *Prayer Power Unlimited.* Chicago: Moody Press, 1977. (A practical guide to personal prayer with useful discusssion questions at the end of each chapter.)

Theresa of Avila. *The Interior Castle.* Translated by Kieran Kavanaugh and Otilio Rodriguez, O.C.D. New York: Paulist Press, 1979. (Written by a sixteenth-century Spanish Carmelite, this book describes seven inward dwelling places into which the soul enters through the gateway of prayer, and in the seventh, which is in the center, God dwells in the greatest splendor.)

4. THE DISCIPLINE OF FASTING

The central idea in fasting is the voluntary denial of an otherwise normal function for the sake of intense spiritual activity. There is nothing wrong with any normal life-functions; it is simply that there are times when we set them aside in order to concentrate. When we view fasting from this perspective, we can see its reasonableness as well as its broader dimensions. The Bible deals with fasting in regard to food, but allow me to take the central principle and apply it to other aspects of contemporary culture.*

First, there is a need today to learn to fast from people. We have a tendency to devour people, and we usually get severe heartburn as a result. I suggest that we must learn to fast from people not because we are antisocial, but precisely because we love people intently and because, when we are with them, we want to be able to do them good and not harm. The Discipline of solitude and the Discipline of community go hand in hand. Until we have learned to be alone, we cannot be with people in a way that will help them, for we will bring to that relationship our own scatteredness. Conversely, until we have learned to be with people, being alone will be a dangerous thing, for it will cut us off from hurting, bleeding humanity.

Second, let us learn to fast from the media at times. It has always amazed me that many people seem incapable (or at least unwilling) to go through an entire day while concentrating on a single thing. Their train of thought is constantly broken up by this demand and that—the newspaper, the radio, the television, the magazines. No wonder so many people feel fractured and fragmented. Obviously, there is a time for the media, but there is also a time to be without

---

*Some of the following ideas have appeared in a somewhat different form in another book of mine, *Freedom of Simplicity* (San Francisco: Harper & Row, 1981), pp. 138–139.

28

the media. Parents send their children to summer camp and the children come back thrilled because "God spoke to me!" What happened at camp was this: they simply were freed of enough distractions for a long enough period of time that they were able to concentrate. We too can do that through the course of our ordinary days.

Third, I would suggest times of fasting from the telephone. The telephone is a wonderful invention, but it must not control us. I have known people who stop praying in order to answer the telephone! I want to let you in on a secret: you are under no obligation to answer that gadget every time it rings. In our home, when we are eating or when I am reading stories to the children, we do not answer the telephone because I want my boys to know they are more important than any phone call. And it is terribly offensive to interrupt an important conversation just to answer a machine.

Fourth, I would like to suggest the Discipline of fasting from billboards. I still remember the day I was driving on the Los Angeles freeway system when, all of a sudden, I realized that for one solid hour my mind had been dominated by the billboards. Now when I suggest that we fast from billboards, I do not mean that we should refrain from looking at them. But I do suggest that the billboard should become a signal to us of another reality. When the ad man shouts his four-letter obscenity, "More, more, more," let it remind us of another four-letter word, a rich, full-bodied word, "Less, less, less." When we are bombarded with bigger-than-life pictures of foxy ladies and well-fed babies, perhaps we can use those pictures to trigger in our minds another world, a world in which 460 million people are the victims of acute hunger (ten thousand of them will be dead by this time tomorrow), a world in which a million hogs in Indiana have superior housing to a billion people on this planet.

This leads me to my fifth and final suggestion concerning fasting, which is that we discover times to fast from our gluttonous consumer culture that we find so comfortable. For our soul's sake, we need times when we go among Christ's favorites—the broken, the bruised, the dispossessed—not to preach to them, but to learn from them. For the sake of our balance, our sanity, we need times when we are among those who, in the words of Mahatma Gandhi, live an "eternal compulsory fast."

Fasting is a Spiritual Discipline ordained by God for the good of

29

the Christian fellowship. May God find our hearts open to this means of receiving grace.

Daily Scripture Readings

Sunday: The example of Christ / Luke 4:1–13.

Monday: God's chosen fast / Isaiah 58:1–7.

Tuesday: A partial fast / Daniel 10:1–14.

Wednesday: A normal fast / Nehemiah 1:4–11.

Thursday: An absolute fast / Esther 4:12–17.

Friday: The inauguration of the gentile mission / Acts 13: 1–3.

Saturday: The appointment of elders in the churches / Acts 14:19–23.

Study Questions

1. Check your first reaction to the thought of fasting:
   _____ ugh
   _____ hmmm
   _____ wow!
   _____ ok
   _____ freedom
   _____ you have to be kidding
2. How does Christian fasting differ from the hunger strike and health fasting?
3. Define "a normal fast," "a partial fast," and "an absolute fast."
4. What is the primary purpose of fasting?
5. How can fasting reveal what controls your life?
6. What is most difficult about fasting for you?
7. Fast for two meals (twenty-four hours) and give the time saved to God. Record anything you learn from the experience.
8. Try fasting from the media for one week and see what you learn about yourself during that time.
9. Consider whether fasting is a cultural expression of Christian

faith only or whether it is an expression of faith for all cultures at all times.

10. In his day, John Wesley required that every minister ordained in the Methodist Church regularly fast two days a week. Discuss the implications that such a requirement would have in our day.

Suggested Books for Further Study

Cartwright, Thomas. *The Holy Exercise of a True Fast.* London: 1610. (Written by a Puritan leader who was the first minister in England, after the Reformation, to make clear the important distinction between fasting for health purposes and fasting for spiritual purposes.)

Ehret, Arnold. *Rational Fasting.* Beaumont, Tex.: Ehret Literature Publishing Co., 1971. (A consideration of fasting from the perspective of physical health and well-being.)

Knox, John. *Order and Doctrine of a General Fast.* Edinburgh: 1565. (Written by the leader of the Scottish Reformation.)

Prince, Derek. *Shaping History through Prayer and Fasting.* Old Tappan, N.J.: Fleming H. Revell Co., 1973. (Filled with many interesting historical examples, this study by a leader in the charismatic movement seeks to show the impact of fasting upon societies.)

Rogers, Eric N. *Fasting: The Phenomenon of Self Denial.* Nashville, Tenn.: Thomas Nelson Inc., 1976. (A survey of fasting among the great religions of the world, including a study of fasting for political and health purposes.)

Smith, David R. *Fasting.* Fort Washington, Penn.: Christian Literature Crusade, 1969. (An excellent study that includes the best bibliography to be had on fasting.)

Smith, Fred W. *Journal of a Fast.* New York: Ballantine Books, 1972. (The journal notations of a blue-collar worker who undertook an extended fast. It is filled with human interest and practical wisdom, even though you may find some of his philosophical and theological comments strange.)

Wallis, Arthur. *God's Chosen Fast.* Fort Washington, Penn.: Christian Literature Crusade, 1971. (In my opinion, the best single book on the market today that brings together the theory and the practice of Christian fasting.)

5. THE DISCIPLINE OF STUDY

The mind will always take on an order that conforms to the order of whatever it concentrates upon. Once some friends let us use their beach house on the Oregon coast. Its location was a secluded spot where virtually the only building in sight was an old light house on a far peninsula. Our only visitors were seagulls. The cabin had no television and no telephone. Even the radio didn't work. But there were a record player and two old records—the sound tracks from *Oklahoma!* and *Johnny Appleseed.* "How nice," I thought. "One record for the children and one for the adults." In the course of a week, we must have played those two records some fifty times. For months afterward, I found myself singing or humming the songs on those albums—in the shower, in board meetings, in church. I even sang them in my dreams. What happened was simple: the functioning of my mind had taken on the order of the music.

This is why the problem of mind pollution is so crucial. Now when I speak of mind pollution, I am not thinking only of "bad" books, movies, and so forth, but of the mediocre ones as well. You see, unless we set before ourselves an "habitual vision of greatness," we will surely degenerate. This is why it is ruinous that so much of our Christian literature is of such poor literary quality. The sad fact of the modern world is that, in the main, men do not read at all, and many women are captives to the escape romance novel, which is of such poor quality that it should not even be considered literature. We simply must raise our sights.

Have you ever pondered why people in our day do not read? Certainly, we do not lack the time. In 1981, we spent seventy-five thousand man-years playing video games* and God knows how

---

*"Alien Creatures in the Home," *Time* magazine, January 18, 1982, p. 57.

many more thousands (or millions?) entranced by television. Though I have yet to join the video-game craze (I'm too self-conscious), I certainly don't mind a television program now and then. On the other hand, abject slavery is another thing altogether. This week, my son's fifth-grade teacher polled the members of the class on their weekend activities and found that the majority of the class watched over fifteen hours of television and read under one hour. Only one other student besides Joel had watched less than two hours of television and had read for about seven hours.

In order to raise our sights and take the Spiritual Discipline of study seriously, may I put in a plug for disciplined reading. In my courses at the university, I usually require seven or eight books in each class. At first, students think they are being sent to the guillotine, but by the end of the term, they are thrilled to discover such a rich world, a world that makes "pac man" or "The Dukes of Hazzard" look drab and dull.

Our children are required to read each evening. Both boys go to their room at 8:00 P.M. (Notice, this means that we must say no to most evening church meetings and entertainment extravaganzas, though we will make rare exceptions.) Joel, our ten-year-old, is allowed to read for one hour. Nathan, our seven-year-old, reads for fifteen minutes. And with only minimal encouragement from us, they have gotten into some substantial literature—Joel is presently devouring *The Lord of the Rings*. We also read together out loud. Recently, Nathan has requested *The Chronicles of Narnia* and so (although Joel has read this collection many times) we all sit together after supper and share in the wonderful adventures that take place in the magical land of Narnia. Next we plan to read aloud *The Pilgrim's Progress*.

Study, of course, is a much larger Discipline than reading, and many who read never study; but reading is an important element in study and should not be lost. I'm sure you will find God waiting for you as you engage in the ministry of study.

Daily Scripture Readings

Sunday: The call to study / Proverbs 1:1–9, 23:12, 23.

Monday: The source of truth / James 1:5, Hebrews 4:11–13, 2 Timothy 3:16–17.

33

Tuesday: What to study / Philippians 4:8–9, Colossians 3:1–17.

Wednesday: The value of study / Luke 10:38–42.

Thursday: Active study / Ezra 7:10, James 1:19–25.

Friday: Study in the evangelistic enterprise / Acts 17:1–3, 17:10–12, 19:8–10.

Saturday: The study of a nonverbal book / Proverbs 24:30–34.

Study Questions

1. Why does study more fully bring about the purpose of the Spiritual Disciplines, which is the transformation of the individual? In other words, what does study do that other Disciplines do not?
2. What is study? (This is an important question, because so many Christians do not know its answer.)
3. Have you had any experience with the study of nonverbal books?
4. The four steps into study that I give are repetition, concentration, comprehension, and reflection. Which of these four steps do you feel is the most important in bringing about the goal of the transformation of the individual?
5. Outside of the Bible, what book has had the most profound impact upon your own life? Why?
6. On page 60 of *Celebration*, I write, "In study we are not seeking spiritual ecstasy; in fact, ecstasy can be a hindrance." How could spiritual ecstasy be a hindrance?
7. List three things that you could do this next week in order to follow the dictum of Socrates: know thyself.
8. Study a plant or tree for ten minutes and then write down what you learn from the experience.
9. Why does study produce joy?
10. Consider the purchase of a serious book on the spiritual life to read this next week.

Suggested Books for Further Study

Adler, Mortimer J. *How to Read a Book*. New York: Simon and

34

Schuster, 1958. (The standard by which all of us measure our efforts. Essential reading for all who want to read correctly.)

Blamires, Harry. *The Christian Mind*. Ann Arbor, Mich.: Servant Books, 1963. (A careful analysis of the assumptions of the contemporary culture and a call to a more authentic Christian world view by a former student of C. S. Lewis.)

Rutherford, Jean, et al. *How to Study the Bible*. Edited by John B. Job. Downers Grove, Ill.: InterVarsity Press, 1972. (Presents some eight approaches to Bible study, including character study, word study, and theme study.)

Sire, James E. *How to Read Slowly: A Christian Guide to Reading with the Mind*. Downers Grove, Ill.: InterVarsity Press, 1979. (Helps Christians read so that the world view of the author becomes obvious.)

Stott, John R. W. *Understanding the Bible*. Grand Rapids, Mich.: Zondervan Publishing House, 1982. (An exceedingly helpful resource for personal Bible study covering issues of interpretation and authority as well as the basic flow of the Biblical story.)

Trueblood, Elton. *The New Man for Our Time*. New York: Harper & Row, 1970. (A plea for Christians to love God with their minds as well as their hearts and their hands.)

PART II

The Outward Disciplines

6. THE DISCIPLINE OF SIMPLICITY

Simplicity is openness, unselfconsciousness, naturalness. It is the opposite of subtlety, cunning, duplicity.

Where simplicity abounds, words can be taken at face value: there is no hidden agenda. And yet, simplicity is not synonymous with "easy to understand." Jesus was not easy to understand nor was Paul, but both were characterized by simplicity of speech. Their intent was not to confuse or deceive but to clarify and illuminate.

Simplicity frees us from the tyranny of the self, the tyranny of things, and the tyranny of people.*

The self clamors for attention, self-recognition, applause. Through artful deception, it appears to be younger, wiser, richer, saintlier than is actually the case. The self will go to extravagant lengths to seem to belong to the intelligentsia. In meetings, it will quote authors it has never read or maintain a discreet silence in supposed superiority over so uneducated a group.

Confront and challenge the tyranny of the self with the following questions:

—Am I pretending to be an expert where I am only an amateur?
—Do I really read the books I quote?
—Do I use rhetoric as a curtain to conceal my true intentions?
—Do I give the impression of being more godly (or more profane, whichever will give more status in the group) than I truly am?
—Do I try to impress people with my degrees, titles, or honors?

Simplicity also prevails against the tyranny of things. Out of fear that others might discover who we are, we create an artificial world of ostentatious display, extravagant ornamentation, and preten-

_____
*These brief words are adopted from material in Albert Day's book, *Discipline and Discovery.*

39

tious style. We call upon the beautician, the tailor, and the dressmaker to create an impression of perpetual youth. We buy clothes, cars, and houses beyond our means in a frantic attempt to appear successful.

Rebuke the tyranny of things with the following questions:

—Am I living contentedly within my income?
—Do I act my age?
—Am I a compulsive buyer?
—Do I try to impress people with gadgets?
—Do I buy what I can afford and what my responsibility to the poor suggests?

Finally, there is the tryanny of people. What horrendous gymnastics we will put ourselves through just to insure that others will have a good opinion of us. How desperately and sincerely we labor to create the right impression. Instead of becoming good, we resort to all sorts of devices to make people think we are good.

Joyfully attack the tyranny of people with the following questions:

—Can I allow an unfavorable comment about myself to stand, without any need to straighten out the matter?
—In recounting events, do I shift the story ever so slightly to make myself appear in a more favorable light?
—Must I always make excuses for my behavior?
—Do I aim at excellence in my work without regard for what people may say or think?
—Can I accept compliments freely without any need to shrug them off in self-conscious modesty?

Only the simple are free. All others are tyrannized by the ambitious self, the demand for recognition through things, and a preoccupation with the opinions of others. François Fénelon declared, "Simplicity is an uprightness of soul which prevents self-consciousness. Verily such simplicity is a great treasure!"

Daily Scripture Readings

Sunday: Simplicity as singleness of heart / Matthew 6:19–24.

40

Monday: Simplicity as trust / Matthew 6:25–34.

Tuesday: Simplicity as obedience / Genesis 15.

Wednesday: The generosity of simplicity / Leviticus 25:8–12.

Thursday: Simplicity in speech / Matthew 5:33–37, James 5:12.

Friday: Simplicity and justice / Amos 5:11–15, 24, Luke 4:16–21.

Saturday: The freedom from covetousness / Luke 12:13–34.

Study Questions

1. What are the two aspects of simplicity and why are *both* essential?
2. In one paragraph, attempt to set forth the biblical teaching on possessions.
3. What would the concept of the year of Jubilee look like in a modern society (Lev. 25:8–12)?
4. What do I set forth as the focal point for an understanding of Christian simplicity?
5. What are the three inward attitudes of simplicity? Of the three, which do you find the most difficult for you personally?
6. What is the greatest danger in setting forth an outward expression to Christian simplicity? Why *must* we take the risk?
7. Which of the ten controlling principles for outward simplicity is the most helpful to you? Are there any you feel are unrealistic?
8. What is producing an addiction in you?
9. Wrestle with the implications of the ninth principle. (Reject anything that will breed the oppression of others.)
10. List one thing that you could do this next week to simplify your life. Do it.

Suggested Books for Further Study

Cooper, John C. *Finding a Simpler Life*. Philadelphia: United Church Press, 1974. (Lays the groundwork for an authentic vision of simplicity in modern society.)

41

Cooper, John C. *The Joy of the Plain Life*. Nashville, Tenn.: Impact Books, 1981. (A joyous celebration of the gift of simplicity. Cooper has made his book particularly helpful by having individuals from many walks of life share at the end of each chapter their practical experiences of the chapter theme.)

Edwards, Tilden. *Living Simply through the Day*. New York: Paulist Press, 1977. (Beginning with a personal pilgrimage, Edwards helps to free us from our anxiety-ridden culture by simple exercises that are tied to our daily experiences of eating, playing, serving, sleeping, etc.)

Eller, Vernard. *The Simple Life*. Grand Rapids, Mich.: Eerdmans Publishing Co., 1973. (A look at inward simplicity through the eyes of the gospel records and in the writings of Søren Kierkegaard.)

Foster, Richard. *Freedom of Simplicity*. San Francisco: Harper & Row, 1981. (Attempts to place simplicity within the context of the whole of Christian devotion and to bring together the various emphases upon inner and outer simplicity.)

Gish, Arthur G. *Beyond the Rat Race*. New Canaan, Conn.: Keats Publishing, 1973. (Gish launches an uncompromising attack on materialism and a vigorous call to outward simplicity that is guaranteed to disturb you to the core.)

Hengel, Martin. *Property and Riches in the Early Church*. Philadelphia: Fortress Press, 1974. (A scholarly study of the Christian approach to property and riches from the time of Christ—with a brief discussion of Old Testament views—to about the fourth century. Extensive attention is given to the Ante-Nicene Fathers.)

Longacre, Doris Janzen. *Living More with Less*. Scottsdale, Ariz.: Herald Press, 1980. (A follow-up to her bestselling *More-With-Less Cookbook*. This volume is filled with a wealth of practical suggesions by Mennonites throughout the world.)

Sider, Ronald J. *Rich Christians in an Age of Hunger: A Biblical Study*. Downers Grove, Ill.: InterVarsity Press, 1979. (Extremely valuable biblical and practical study of the question of justice in modern society. Must reading.)

Taylor, Richard K. *Economics and the Gospel*. Philadelphia: United Church Press, 1973. (A powerful analysis of economic justice in the context of Christian ethics.)

42

Ziegler, Edward K. *Simple Living*. Elgin, Ill.: The Brethren Press, 1974. (A look at simplicity from the perspective of the Church of the Brethren.)

7. THE DISCIPLINE OF SOLITUDE

Henri Nouwen has noted that "without solitude it is virtually impossible to lead a spiritual life." Why is this so? Because, in solitude, we are freed *from* our bondage to people and our inner compulsions, and we are freed *to* love God and know compassion for others.

To enter solitude, we must disregard what others think of us. Who will understand this call to aloneness? Even our closest friends will see it as a terrible waste of precious time and as rather selfish and self-centered. But, oh, what liberty is released in our hearts when we let go of the opinions of others! The less we are mesmerized by human voices, the more we are able to hear the divine Voice. The less we are bound by other's expectations, the more we are open to God's expectations.

But, in solitude, we die not only to others but also to ourselves. To be sure, at first we thought solitude was a way to recharge our batteries in order to enter life's many competitions with new vigor and strength. In time, however, we found that solitude did not give us power to win the rat race; on the contrary, it taught us to ignore the struggle altogether. Slowly, we found ourselves letting go of our inner compulsions to win and our frantic effort to attain. In the stillness, our false, busy selves were unmasked and seen for the imposters they truly were.

It is out of our liberation from others and self that our ears become open to hear and our eyes unveiled to see the goodness of God. We can love God because we do not have to love the world. Through our solitude, an open inner space has been created through which God finds us. In solitude, we experience a second (and third, and fourth, and fifth . . .) conversion. In a deeper more profound way, we turn from the idols of the marketplace to the glory of God in the

44

face of Jesus Christ. God takes this "useless" Discipline, this "wasted time," to make us His friend.

A happy by-product of becoming the friend of God is an increased compassion for others. Once we have peered into the abyss of our own vanity, we can never again look at the struggles of others in condescending superiority. Once we have faced the demons of despair in our own aloneness, we can never again pass off lightly the quiet depression and sad loneliness of those we meet. We become one with all who hurt and are afraid. We are free to give them the greatest gift we possess—the gift of ourselves.

The private retreat is one way to nurture solitude. In *Celebration*, I shared several ideas regarding what to do in a private retreat; however, it is of utmost importance that we do not lose sight of our major work on retreat. It can be said in one word—PRAYER. We enter the terrifying silences to listen to God, to experience communion. This purpose needs to be kept before us because, at first, time thus spent will seem so useless, so wasted. We will soon be severely tempted to make "good use of our time" by reading many books or writing many pages. What we must clearly understand and underscore is that our real task on retreat is to create a space in our lives where God can reach us. Once that space has been created we wait quietly, expectantly. From this point on, the work belongs to God. And I have found Him most eager to usher us into the Holy of Holies and share with us the glories of His Kingdom.

In *Fruits of Solitude*, William Penn observed that solitude is "a school few care to learn in, tho' none instructs us better." May we be among the few that care to learn through this merciful means of God's grace.

Daily Scripture Readings

Sunday: The freedom to control the tongue / James 3:1–12, Luke 23:6–9.

Monday: Prayer and solitude / Matthew 6:5–6, Luke 5:16.

Tuesday: The insights of solitude / Psalm 8.

Wednesday: "The dark night of the soul" / Jeremiah 20:7–18.

Thursday: The solitude of the garden / Matthew 26:36–46.

45

Friday: The solitude of the cross / Matthew 27:32–50.

Saturday: The compassion that comes from solitude / Matthew 9:35–38, 23:37.

Study Questions

1. What is the difference between loneliness and solitude? Which do you experience more?
2. Why do we need both solitude and community in order to function with spiritual success?
3. Why do you think that solitude and silence are closely connected?
4. What is the "sacrifice of fools"? Have you ever been guilty?
5. Have you ever had an experience such as this described by Catherine de Haeck Doherty: "All in me is silent and . . . I am immersed in the silence of God"? If so, you might want to share it with someone; if not, you might want to ponder the reason for the lack.
6. Have you ever experienced a "dark night of the soul"?
7. I mention five possible steps into solitude. Which one would you find most helpful at this point in your life?
8. What keeps you from solitude?
9. What practical reordering of your life could be done in order to create more space for God?
10. What experience in solitude would you like to have two years from now that you do not presently possess? Would you be willing this week to plan it into your schedule for sometime in the next twenty-four months?

Suggested Books for Further Study

Doherty, Catherine de Hueck. *Poustinia: Christian Spirituality of the East for Western Man.* Notre Dame: Ave Maria Press, 1974. (A sensitive and highly applicable discussion of how Western culture can find space for the life of solitude.)

Hoyland, Geoffrey. *The Use of Silence.* Inner Life Series #5. London: S.P.C.K., 1955. (A pamphlet on the Quaker experience of the "Living Silence" on both individual and corporate levels.)

46

Maloney, George A., S.J. *Alone with the Alone*. Notre Dame: Ave Maria Press, 1982. (Helps the individual enter into the experience of God—[the Alone]—through the format of an eight-day retreat.)

Nee, Watchman. *Deep Calleth unto Deep*. Los Angeles: The Stream. (A tiny booklet that beckons you to the inner sanctuary of the soul.)

Nouwen, Henri J. M. *The Genesee Diary*. New York: Doubleday, 1976. (Going from an active life of teaching at Yale Divinity School to a seven-month experience in a Trappist Monastery, Nouwen shares the insights of his sojourn.)

Nouwen, Henri J. M. *Out of Solitude*. Notre Dame: Ave Maria Press, 1974. (Three brief passages on the fruit of solitude in contemporary ministry.)

Nouwen, Henri J. M. *The Way of the Heart*. New York: The Seabury Press, 1981. (A meaningful interpretation into the twentieth century of the wisdom of the Desert Fathers.)

Oats, Wayne. *Nurturing Silence in a Noisy Heart*. New York: Doubleday, 1979. (Most helpful counsel on how inner solitude can take up residence in the midst of our busy lives.)

Waddell, Helen. *The Desert Fathers*. Ann Arbor, Mich.: University of Michigan Press, 1957. (Contains many of the wise sayings of the Desert Fathers as well as the stories of their experiences.)

8. THE DISCIPLINE OF SUBMISSION

In submission, we recognize the legitimate authority of others over us. It is nothing more than the simple understanding that "no man is an island." Life in community is our rightful home: relationships with other human beings is our inheritance. To confess our commitment to community means to confess our commitment to mutual subordination. Peter crystallized this principle in the simple phrase, "Honor all men" (1 Peter 2:17a), and Paul set forth the idea in what must be considered the most memorable sentence on the subject, "Be subject to one another out of reverence for Christ" (Eph. 5:21).

Submission is a concept as broad as life itself and a Discipline found throughout Scripture. It raises issues that are deep and difficult: issues of submission to the ways of God, issues of submission to the state, issues of submission to the Christian fellowship, issues of submission in the Christian household and much more. As we hammer out our understanding of these matters, we will always want to hold before us the life and death of Christ as the divine paradigm by which all the verbs of Christian submission are to be conjugated.

In regard to the Christian family, the New Testament dared to flesh out the meaning of submission in a body of instructions that Martin Luther called the *Haustafeln*, or "The Table of Instructions for the Christian Household."* This teaching was a gracious way of setting forth the function of submission within the family in first century culture. In our day, however, this body of instructions has been terribly garbled and abused. The following distortions of submission reveal in part the knack we moderns have for taking the best teaching and using it for the worst ends.

---

*Eph. 5:21 ff., Col. 3:18 ff., Titus 2:4 ff., and 1 Pet. 2:1 ff.

48

The Doormat. This is the person who allows others to misuse and abuse him to such an extent that he is treated as a thing rather than a person. In a false and unhealthy submission, he allows others to walk over him as one would a doormat. His opinion is neither sought nor desired, and in time he loses the ability even to have an opinion. Such a person soon becomes an object rather than a subject—a housekeeper rather than a wife, a breadwinner rather than a husband. He is defined by what he can produce rather than by who he is. In the end, he becomes a thing.

The Pleaser. This is the person who wants more than anything else to avoid conflict. He sees a fight coming a mile away and will go to any lengths to keep it from occurring. It is comical (and tragic) to find two "pleasers" married to each other:

"What would you like to do tonight, honey?"
"Whatever you would like, dear."
"Well, I just want to make you happy."
"And that is exactly what I want to do for you. I'll do anything that will make you happy."
"If it would please you, I would be glad to go out to dinner."
"I'd love to, if it would make you happy."
"Fine, what kind of food would you like?"
"Whatever you would enjoy, dear."

. . . and on it goes *ad nauseam.*

The Dependent. This is the person who fears making decisions like the plague. Rather than own up to the maturing process of choice, he finds refuge in a pseudo-submission that allows others to make all his decisions. Fear is at the root of such submission—fear of leading others in the wrong way, fear of making an ill-timed decision, fear of blame if programs fail. And so he never causes waves, he never offends, and he never accomplishes anything of lasting value.

The Manipulator. This is the person who follows all of the outward rules of submission, but employs every subtle trick of the trade to get his own way. Acts of mercy are done to put us into his debt. Words of kindness are given to win us to his side. While fully agreeing with our decisions, little hints of doubt are sown through a look or a gesture or perhaps a slight quavering of the voice. Often the

49

practice is so ingrained that the individual himself does not realize that he has taken control of every situation.

The distortions that I have shared here are, for the most part, religiously apporoved means to dehumanizing and destructive ends. But Jesus Christ calls us to a more excellent way—a way of love and compassion, a way of submission and service.

Daily Scripture Readings

Sunday:	The call to submission / Mark 8:34, John 12:24–26.
Monday:	The example of Christ / Philippians 2:1–11.
Tuesday:	The example of Abraham / Genesis 22:1–19.
Wednesday:	The example of Paul / Galatians 2:19–21.
Thursday:	Submission in the marketplace / Matthew 5:38–48.
Friday:	Submission in the family / Ephesians 5:21–6:9, 1 Peter 3:1–9.
Saturday:	Submission with reference to the state / Romans 13:1–10, Acts 4:13–20, 5:27–29, 16:35–39.

Study Questions

1. How have you seen the Discipline of submission abused?
2. What is the freedom in submission? Have you entered into any experience of this?
3. I write, "In submission we are at last free to value other people." What is it about submission that allows this to happen?
4. Why did I begin the chapter by discussing what submission does before I define what it is?
5. What images come to your mind when you think of the word *self-denial*?
6. Why was Jesus' teaching on submission so revolutionary?
7. In one brief paragraph, attempt to summarize what you feel is the teaching of the Epistles on submission.
8. What are the limits of submission, and why are they important?
9. Of the seven acts of submission, which one do you feel you need to work on most?

10. What do you think it would mean to be in submission to the ways of God? (Ponder this question carefully because it does not yield to pat answers.)

Suggested Books for Further Study

The small number of books listed below does not reflect my unawareness of the breadth of contemporary writing, but my unwillingness to commend most of it to you. The idea of submission pervaded the world view of the old writers (think of à Kempis' *Imitation* or Fénelon's *Christian Perfection*), but it is a strange mutation to modern writers. For the most part, contemporary discussions are limited to two small corners of the Discipline—the man/woman question and the Shepherding or Discipling concept in certain charismatic circles. To my knowledge, no one has provided us with a full-blown, intelligent discussion of this subject.

Butt, Howard. *The Velvet Covered Brick*. New York: Harper & Row, 1973. (The experience of one man's attempt to take the biblical concepts of "authority" and "submission" and hammer them out on the hard anvil of the business world.)

Smedes, Lewis B. *Love within Limits*. Grand Rapids, Mich.: William B. Eerdmans Publishing Co., 1978. (Basing his definition upon 1 Corinthians 13, Smedes describes love as "the power that moves us to respond to a neighbor's need with no expectation of reward"; by this description, he defines the fundamental principle out of which the Discipline of submission operates.)

Yoder, John Howard. *The Politics of Jesus*. Grand Rapids, Mich.: Eerdmans Publishing Co., 1972. (Impressive in its scholarship and its insight. Contains two important chapters on the subject: "Revolutionary Subordination" and "Let Every Soul Be Subject: Romans 13 and the Authority of the State." Yoder gives us an excellent foundation for a modern understanding of the Discipline of submission for our day: we now need someone who could build upon it.)

9. THE DISCIPLINE OF SERVICE

In his most famous teaching on service, Jesus concluded, "For even the Son of Man did not come to be served, but to serve, and to give his life a ransom for many" (Mark 10:45, NIV). Our Lord's unique service of redemption through the Cross is unrepeatable. However, we are called to serve through the many little deaths of going beyond self. And as we live out our lives for the good of others, amazingly, we find ourselves, we discover our sense of place.

When Paul spoke of the generosity of the believers in Macedonia, he noted that, "First they gave themselves (2 Cor. 8:5a). This is the first mark of the Discipline of service. Service cannot be done *in absentia*. It necessitates our personal involvement. Like St. Francis of Assisi, we must touch the leper, we must reach out to the one in need.

How counter this is to the modern call to watch out for number one. (And may I just add that if you are driven by the need to watch out for number one, God help you, because no one else will!) But in the Kingdom of God, we can let go of such drives because we are able to cast all our care upon him, for he cares for us (1 Peter 5:7).

One reality must be clearly understood in the life of service. The very fact that we are finite means that if we say yes to one task, then we must say no to other tasks. When I agreed to the service of writing this study guide, I had to turn away many good and noble tasks. I could not go to special meetings, serve on worthy committees, speak at important gatherings, or even counsel with needy people. To have given in to these other important ministries would have meant failing to serve through writing.

Listen to this heartbreaking story of a young mother who in the beginning thought service meant accepting any and all demands upon her time and energy:

52

Someone was *always* dropping in for a visit and staying late, often till 2 A.M. until we were exhausted. We had *no* time to be together as a family. The routine and discipline of our two small children were disturbed to the point that they were being raised by other people while we had Bible studies and shared with needy folk. The relationship between my husband and me suffered because we were exhausted and had very little time alone. I became the dumping place for preschoolers until I was just about berserk from the responsibility. I became the maker of clothes for many of the women who were working outside the home and simply didn't have time to sew. I became "the listener" who spent so much time on the phone that there were *many* days that my children's lunches were fixed from things I could reach from the phone and my housework was untouched due to serving others. And on and on it went until I finally cracked, put my foot down and learned to say "No."

This deeply committed woman was having to say no to her children and husband because she was saying yes to the demands of other folk.

The point is that we are not omnipresent and we should admit as much. The Discipline of service asks us to serve irrespective of class or status distinctions, but it also recognizes our human limitations. Love is a reasoned concern for the well-being of all. If I bring people into my home under the supposition that I am serving them, but in the process I destroy my wife and children, then I am not living in love. Most likely I am merely gratifying my egocentric need to feel righteous rather than entering into true service. Admittedly, the balance is not easy to maintain—significant matters in life seldom are. That is the reason for discipline: remember, the disciplined person is the person who can do what needs to be done when it needs to be done.

Discernment and obedience are the keys. Learning when to say no is important; so is learning when to say yes. Once we have been burned by a compulsive yes, the temptation will be to say no to everything or, at least, to those things we find distasteful. But that can be as enslaving as the former state. What we need is to learn the rhythm of the Holy Spirit so that our yes or no to calls of service will arise out of that harmony.

53

Daily Scripture Readings

Sunday: The call to service / Matthew 20:20–28.

Monday: The sign of service / John 13:1–17.

Tuesday: The commitment of service / Exodus 21:2, 21:5–6, 1 Corinthians 9:19.

Wednesday: The attitude of service / Colossians 3:23–25.

Thursday: Service in the Christian fellowship / Romans 12: 9–13.

Friday: The ministry of small things / Matthew 25:31–39.

Saturday: Service exemplified / Luke 10:29–37.

Study Questions

1. If the towel is the sign of service, how can that sign be manifested in twentieth-century culture?
2. Did you find the discussion of self-righteous service, as contrasted from true service, to be:
   _____ right on
   _____ terribly idealistic
   _____ naive
   _____ faithful to Scripture, but impractical for today
   _____ strange
   Discuss your answer with others.
3. Debate the notion that love is a "reasoned concern for the well-being of all," and consider the implications of this notion with reference to service.
4. In the book I mention that service works humility into our lives. What in the world do you think humility means? That is, what does humility look like?
5. Have you ever allowed yourself to be taken advantage of? Did the experience turn out to be destructive rather than redemptive?
6. Does the believer have rights that should not be given up for the sake of others?
7. What would the service of hiddenness look like in your life?

8. During this next week, see if you can find one way each day to exercise the service of common courtesy.
9. When should you say no to the demands that people place upon your time and attention?
10. Give this prayer a try sometime this month: "Lord Jesus, I would so appreciate it if you would bring me someone today whom I can serve."

Suggested Books for Further Study

Bonhoeffer, Dietrich. *Life Together*. Translated by John W. Doberstein. San Francisco: Harper & Row, 1976. (Powerful insights into the life of service, solitude, and confession. Essential reading.)

Greenleaf, Robert K. *The Servant as Leader*. Cambridge, Mass.: Center for Applied Studies, 1973. (A thirty-seven page essay intended as the first of four pamphlets on service as it relates to individuals, trustees, and institutions.)

Greenleaf, Robert K. *Servant Leadership*. New York: Paulist Press, 1977. (A seminal work on the nature of legitimate power and greatness by one who clearly understands both the world of corporate management and the Christian witness to service.)

Mains, Karen Burton. *Open Heart Open Home*. Elgin, Ill.: David C. Cook Publishing Co., 1981. (An encouraging call to the ministry of Christian hospitality.)

Swindoll, Charles R. *Improving Your Serve*. Waco, Tex.: Word Books, 1981. (Helpful, life-related sermons on the art of unselfish living.)

PART III

The Corporate Disciplines

10. THE DISCIPLINE OF CONFESSION

Confession is a corporate Discipline, because sin both offends God and creates a wound in the Christian fellowship. In the early centuries of the Christian era, forgiveness and reconciliation involved a lengthy process of healing by which the offender was restored to health through the ministry of the total Christian community. In the early Middle Ages, confession was turned increasingly into a private sacrament, and following the Reformation, Protestants began to view is more and more as a matter exclusively between the individual and God. But in the beginning, confession was not the privatistic event it is today; in fact, in Matthew 18, Jesus expressed the essential communal nature of confession and explained how forgiveness can come into a community without destroying the group. It is God who does the forgiving, but often He chooses human beings as the channel of His forgiving grace.

Human beings are such that "life together" always involves them in hurting one another in some way. And forgiveness is essential in a community of hurt and hurtful persons. In experiencing forgiveness, it is important to understand what it is *not*. Four things are often mistaken for forgiveness.

First, some imagine that forgiveness means pretending an injury doesn't really matter. We say, "Oh, that's all right, it really didn't hurt me anyway!" That is not forgiveness; it is lying. And love and lies do not mix well. The truth is that these things matter a great deal, and it does not help to avoid the issue. What we need is not avoidance but reconciliation.

Second, some think that forgiveness means ceasing to hurt. There is the belief that if we continue to hurt we must have failed to forgive completely. That is simply not true. Hurting is not evil. We may hurt for a very long time to come. Forgiveness does not mean

59

that we will stop hurting.

Third, many would have us believe that forgiveness means forgetting. "Forgive and forget," we often say. But the truth of the matter is that we cannot forget. We remember; the difference will be that we no longer need or desire to use the memory against others. The memory remains, the vindictiveness leaves. The attempt to force people to forget what cannot be forgotten only puts them in bondage and confuses the meaning of forgiveness.

Fourth, many assume that forgiveness means pretending that the relationship is just the same as it was before the offense. But this is simply not the case. The relationship will never be the same again. We might just as well make peace with that *fact*. By the grace of God, it may be a hundred times better, but it will never be the same.

True confession and forgiveness bring joy to the Christian community and healing to the parties involved. Most wonderful of all, confession spells reconciliation with God the Father, for as the beloved Apostle said so long ago, "If we confess our sins, he is faithful and just, and will forgive our sins and cleanse us from all unrighteousness" (1 John 1:9).

Daily Scripture Readings

Sunday: The need for confession and forgiveness / Isaiah 59:1–9, Romans 3:10–18.

Monday: The promise of forgiveness / Jeremiah 31:34, Matthew 26:28, Ephesians 1:7.

Tuesday: The assurance of forgiveness / 1 John 1:5–10.

Wednesday: Jesus Christ, our Adequate Savior, Mediator, and Advocate / 2 Timothy 1:8–10, 1 Timothy 2:5, 1 John 2:1.

Thursday: A parable of confession / Luke 15:11–24.

Friday: Authority and forgiveness / Matthew 16:19, 18:18, John 20:23.

Saturday: The ministry of the Christian Fellowship / James 5:13–16.

60

Study Questions

1. In your own words, try to describe the theology that lies behind the Discipline of confession.
2. What are the three advantages to formalized confession? Are there disadvantages?
3. I mention three things that are necessary for a good confession. Which of the three do you find most difficult to experience?
4. What does the idea of living "under the Cross" mean in reference to confession?
5. List two or three dangers that you could imagine would accompany the exercise of the Christian Discipline of confession.
6. Does absolution indicate the forgiveness of sins or does it effect it?
7. When is the Discipline of confession an unhealthy preoccupation with sin and when is it a proper recognition of our need for forgiveness?
8. How would you distinguish between false guilt and genuine guilt?
9. St. Augustine calls the sacraments of baptism and communion the *verba visibilia* (visible words) of our forgiveness, and John Stott notes, "Baptism, being unique and unrepeatable, is the sacrament of our once-for-all justification: Holy Communion, being repeatedly enjoyed, is the sacrament of our daily forgiveness. By them we are assured, audibly and visibly, of our acceptance and forgiveness." What is your reaction to this idea?
10. Sometime this week spend fifteen minutes in silence before God and invite Him to reveal anything within you that needs to be confessed.

Suggested Books for Further Study

Augsburger, David. *Caring Enough to Forgive*. Ventura, Calif.: Regal Books, 1981. (A forceful and perceptive discussion not only of the value of true forgiveness but of the destructiveness of false forgiveness.)

Betz, Otto, ed. *Making Sense of Confession*. Chicago, Ill.: Franciscan Herald Press, 1969. (From a Roman Catholic perspective, this work offers helpful suggestions on how children and teen-

61

agers are nurtured in the Discipline of confession.)

Cornwall, Judson. *Let Us Enjoy Forgiveness*. Old Tappan, N.J.: Fleming H. Revell Co., 1978. (A very readable study of divine forgiveness and exactly how that sets us free to love God and enjoy him forever.)

Haring, Bernard. *Shalom: Peace. The Sacrament of Reconciliation*. New York: Image Books, 1969. (A vigorous description of the sacrament of penance from a Roman Catholic perspective.)

Scanlan, Michael T.O.R. *The Power in Penance: Confession and the Holy Spirit*. Notre Dame: Ave Maria Press, 1972. (A powerful little booklet that brings fresh vitality to an ancient practice in the Catholic church as a result of the charismatic renewal.)

Schlink, M. Basilea. *Repentance: The Joy-Filled Life*. Grand Rapids, Mich.: Zondervan Publishing House, 1973. (A slender but helpful work by the leader of the Mary Sisterhood, a Lutheran order in Germany.)

Stott, John R. W. *Confess Your Sins*. Waco, Tex.: Word Books, 1974. (An extrenely helpful discussion of the forms of confession as well as the meaning of reconciliation by the leading evangelical Anglican of our day.)

11. THE DISCIPLINE OF WORSHIP

We are told that, on one occasion, St. Francis of Assisi "rejoiced greatly in Spirit, and he raised his face toward Heaven and stood for a long time with his mind absorbed in God." He entered worship.

Caught up into God, Juliana of Norwich exclaimed, "I saw Him, and sought Him: and I had Him, I wanted Him. . . . He will be seeing and He will be sought: He will be abided and He will be trusted." She entered worship.

Worship is something that happens. It is experience. When we speak of having a "worship service," we are usually referring to the various elements of worship—hymns, Scripture readings, preaching, Holy Communion, liturgy. All of these may *lead* to worship, but worship is much more than any of these expressions. The expressions are important because they are the means of God's grace, but it is quite possible to do them all without entering into worship.

Worship centers in the experience of reality. Whatever ushers us into the Divine Presence should be welcomed. Whatever hinders a genuine encounter with the living Christ should be shunned. The biblical requirements for worship include such matters as confession, adoration, and proclamation, but the Bible does not hold us to any universal wineskin or form in which worship must be contained. What we are to be committed to is reality—real worship, real confession, real praise, real adoration. If particular forms at particular times bring us more fully into worship, we are free to use them; if not, too bad for the forms. We are free to use the highest liturgy, no form at all, or anything in between so long as it brings us into real worship. The forms of worship must always be subject to the reality of worship.

Christ alone is the leader of worship, and it is He who decides what is needed and when it is needed. We should recognize and

63

welcome the free exercise of all the spiritual gifts, as they are used and directed by the Spirit. Christ puts His Word in the mouth of whomever He chooses, and He confirms this same Word in the hearts of the members of His community. If there is any excess, He will raise up a prophet to bring the needed correction.

All these lofty words about the priority of reality over forms may make you think that I have little use for worship forms. Nothing could be farther from the truth. Worship forms are essential if we are to inflesh the reality of worship. As long as we are finite, we must have forms. And so we bring our bodies, minds, and spirits before God to give Him the glory due His name. We offer the sacrifice of our lips—our singing, our praising, our preaching, our confessing. We offer Him the sacrifice of our bodies—our listening hearts, our eucharistic celebration, our obedient lives. And it is important to do these things whether we feel like doing them or not. Often I come into a worship experience and must honestly confess, "Lord, I do not feel like worshipping, I do not feel righteous, I'm tired and distracted in both body and spirit, but I want to give you this time. This hour belongs to you. I love you and to the best of my ability want to give you the glory due Your name. Therefore, I will sing and pray and listen and ask that in Your mercy You will free my spirit to worship you." And as I do this, often something seems to let go inside: perhaps it is the release of an old fear, or a little bitterness, or maybe just a tight-fisted determination to come into God. When this happens, then the singing of hymns, the reading of Scripture, the confession of sin, the preaching of the Word, the receiving of Communion lead me into praise and adoration, which in turn open the inner sanctuary of the soul into worship.

In this context may I lift up one form of worship that has a very ancient tradition but has fallen on hard times in our century. It is the use of the dance. For a thousand years, Christians did a simple dance movement called the *tripudium* to many of their hymns. It worked well with any song in 2/2, 3/4, or 4/4 time. As they sang, worshippers would take three steps forward, one step back, three steps forward, one step back. In doing this, Christians were actually proclaiming a theology with their feet. They were declaring Christ's victory in an evil world, a victory that moves the church forward but not without setbacks. This simple way to worship with the body can be used in any number of informal worship settings. It can even be done in the sanctuary provided the aisles are wide enough to accommodate three or four abreast, and then worshippers can march around the sanctuary singing the great hymns of the faith.

Above all, worship leads us to Christ the Center, as Bernard of Clairvaux put it so well:

> Jesus, Thou Joy of Loving hearts!
> Thou Fount of life! Thou Light of men!
> From the best bliss that earth imparts,
> We turn unfilled to Thee again.

Daily Scripture Readings

Sunday: Worship in spirit and truth / John 4:19–24.

Monday: Communion: the essence of worship / John 6:52–58, 6:63.

Tuesday: The life of worship / Ephesians 5:18–20, Colossians 3:16–17.

Wednesday: The Lord high and lifted up / Isaiah 6:1–8.

Thursday: Sing to the Lord / Psalm 96.

Friday: Worship of all creation / Psalm 148.

Saturday: Worthy is the Lamb / Revelation 5:6–14.

Study Questions

1. How can we cultivate "holy expectancy"?
2. In the book I say that "God is actively seeking worshipers." Have you had any sense of God as the "Hound of Heaven" seeking you out and drawing you into fellowship and communion with Him?
3. The seventeenth-century Quaker theologian, Robert Barclay, spoke of the Quaker worship experience of being "gathered in the power of the Lord." He was obviously referring to more than the fact that they had come together in the same room. Discuss what the phrase might mean and once you agree on the meaning, consider what could be done to encourage a fuller sense of that experience in your local church.

65

4. Which forms of worship you have experienced have been especially meaningful to you? Do you have any sense of why these particular forms have been more meaningful than others?
5. Critique my rather bold statement that the Bible does not bind us to any universal form (that is, wineskin) of worship. Can you think of any worship forms that should be universally binding upon all cultures of Christians at all times?
6. What advantages or disadvantages do you see in the formalized liturgy used in churches like the Episcopal church as opposed to the more informal worship forms used in churches like the Southern Baptist church?
7. If we truly believe that Christ is alive and present among His people in all His offices, what practical difference would that make in our approach to worship?
8. Do you think experiences of Divine ecstasy are central to worship, peripheral to worship, or destructive to worship?
9. What covenant can you make that will open the door to worship more effectively for you?
10. I write, "Just as worship begins in Holy Expectancy it ends in Holy Obedience." What does that mean for you this next week?

Suggested Books for Further Study

Adams, Doug. *Congregational Dancing in Christian Worship.* Austin, Tex.: The Sharing Co., 1971. (Gives a discussion of the history of dance in the church.)

Emswiler, Thomas Neufer, and Sharon Neufer Emswiler. *Wholeness in Worship.* San Francisco: Harper & Row, 1980. (Contemporary and practical. It can bring fire to worship that is overly rationalistic and depth to worship that has focused upon feelings.)

Kelly, Thomas. *The Eternal Promise.* New York: Harper & Row, 1966. (Kelly's essay, "The Gathered Meeting," which is contained in this book, is probably the most powerful Quaker statement on worship in the twentieth century.)

Nee, Watchman. *Assembling Together.* New York: Christian Fellowship Publishers, 1973. (Practical instruction in the life of worship.)

Steere, Douglas V. *Prayer and Worship*. New York: Association Press, 1940. (An intimate discussion of private and public worship by a contemporary giant on the devotional life.)

Underhill, Evelyn. *Worship*. Westport: Hyperion Press, 1980. (A standard by an important figure among the devotional writers.)

White, James F. *Christian Worship in Transition*. Nashville, Tenn.: Abindgon, 1976. (Provides substantial historical and theological roots for worship.)

White, James F. *New Forms of Worship*. Nashville, Tenn.: Abingdon, 1971. (Practical guidance for those planning worship by one who teaches Christian worship at Perkins School of Theology.)

12. THE DISCIPLINE OF GUIDANCE

Guidance is the most radical of the Disciplines because it goes to the heart of this matter of walking with God. Guidance means the glorious life of hearing God's voice and obeying His word.

The goal of guidance is not specific instructions about this or that matter but conformity to the image of Christ. Paul said, "Those whom he foreknew he predestined to be conformed to the image of his son" (Romans 8:28b). Specific guidance in particular matters is a happy by-product of this goal having worked its way into our lives.

We make such a mystery out of the matter of the will of God. The surest sign that it is God's will for us to be where we are is simply that we are there. Now if we throw that away, we throw away the sovereignty of God over our lives. When we can come to the place where we understand that where we are is holy ground, we will begin to understand the meaning of guidance.

The will of God is discovered as we become acquainted with God, learn His ways, and become His friend. As we do this, God will take us right where we are and produce in us the winsome fruit of love, joy, peace, patience, kindness, goodness, faithfulness, gentleness, and self-control (Gal. 5:22–23). As the friendship grows, as the conformity grows, we will know instinctively what actions would please Him, what decisions would be in accord with His way. Just like our intimate knowledge of and love for our wife or husband guides us to decisions we know they would approve, so our inward fellowship gives an inward knowledge of the ways of God.

There are, of course, the outward tests of God's guidance such as Scripture, the Christian community, divine providence working through circumstance, and our own personal integrity. There are also the exceptional means of guidances such as fleeces, dreams, visions, signs, and angels. It is important for us to remember that

God will not lead us in ways that are contrary to His known will. The Spirit that inspired the Scripture will lead us in ways consistent with the Scripture. Our understanding of God's ways is shaped and tempered by His self-revelation to us in the Bible.

We must also remember that there is such a thing as supernatural guidance that is not divine in origin. John the Beloved warns us to "test the spirits to see whether they are of God" (1 John 4:1). There are principalities and powers who wage war against the Kingdom of God, and they are both real and dangerous.

And so we are not to listen to every voice that comes our way, but only to the voice of the true Shepherd. But here is the wonder of it all. For, as Jesus reminded us, He is the Good Shepherd and His sheep know His voice (John 10:4). We walk in the light, we fulfill his commandments, we put on the mind of Christ, and as we do, we find the voice of the true Shepherd quite different from all imposters. While Satan may push and condemn, Christ draws and encourages, and it is His voice that we obey.

Daily Scripture Readings

Sunday: The polestar of faith / Hebrews 11.

Monday: The guidance of divine Providence / Genesis 24: 1–21.

Tuesday: The guidance of justice and obedience / Isaiah 1:17, 18–20.

Wednesday: Led into all truth / Proverbs 3:5–6, John 14:6, 16:13, Acts 10:1–35.

Thursday: Closed doors, open doors / Acts 16:6–10, 2 Corinthians 2:12.

Friday: Listening or resisting? / Acts 21:8–14.

Saturday: The family likeness / Romans 8:14, 28–30.

Study Questions

1. Is the idea of guidance as a *corporate* Discipline new or strange to you?

69

2. What do you think I mean by the term *the Apostolic Church of the Spirit*? (Note: I am trying to give a rather different twist to the old concept of "Apostolic Succession.")
3. Do you believe that this Spirit-led, Spirit-intoxicated, Spirit-empowered people have already been gathered, or are yet to be gathered in our century?
4. Do you think that the notion of a people under the direct theocratic rule of God is workable, or is it only an illusionary pipe-dream? Am I reading the history of the early church through rose-colored glasses?
5. In what sense does the contemporary charismatic movement approximate or fall short of this vision of a gathered people of the Spirit?
6. What are some of the dangers of corporate guidance?
7. What do you understand the idea of a "spiritual director" to mean? Are there dangers to the idea? Are there advantages to the idea?
8. How should the idea of guidance influence the ways in which we carry on business in our churches? If we believed in guidance, how might it change our present church polity?
9. Have you ever seen the idea of corporate guidance used in destructive ways? What lessons were you able to learn from that experience?
10. If living in guidance comes about mainly through entering into friendship with God so that we know and desire His ways, what should you drop from your life and what should you add to your life in order to deepen your intimacy with Christ?

Suggested Books for Further Study

Edwards, Tilden. *Spiritual Friend*. New York: Paulist Press, 1980. (Sensitive and sane counsel on reclaiming the gift of Spiritual Direction.)

Elliot, Elisabeth. *A Slow and Certain Light*. Nashville, Tenn.: Abingdon Press, 1973. (A slender volume filled with meaningful and mature counsel.)

Leech, Kenneth. *Soul Friend*. San Francisco: Harper & Row, 1977. (Provides a superb history of Spiritual Direction and links it to the best of contemporary psychology.)

70

Mumford, Bob. *Take Another Look at Guidance.* Plainfield, N.J.: Logos International, 1971. (Wise and practical instruction from a leader in the charismatic movement.)

Nebe, August. *Luther as Spiritual Adviser.* Translated by C. A. Hay and C. E. Hay. Philadelphia: 1894. (Helps us to understand Luther in the great tradition of Spiritual Directors.)

Smith, Blaine M. *Knowing God's Will: Biblical Principles on Guidance.* Downers Grove, Ill.: InterVarsity Press, 1979. (Helpful commonsense counsel on guidance with an especially valuable section on the process of decision-making.)

St. John of the Cross. *The Dark Night of the Soul.* New York: Image Books, 1959. (A classic on the spiritual life showing God's guidance and teaching in the experiences of hiddenness and stillness.)

13. THE DISCIPLINE OF CELEBRATION

The Psalmist exclaimed, "Our mouth was filled with laughter, and our tongue with shouts of joy" (Ps. 126:2a). And St. Augustine echoed Scripture's words with the declaration, "A Christian should be an alleluia from head to foot." Celebration is a happy characteristic of those who walk cheerfully over the earth in the power of the Lord.

The joy of the Lord is not merely a good feeling. It is acquainted with suffering and sorrow, heartache and pain. It is not found through seeking. It does not come by trying to pump up the right emotions, nor by having a cheery disposition, nor by attempting to be an optimist.

Joy is the result of provision, place, and personality functioning properly in the course of our daily lives. It comes as a result of the abundant life Jesus promised having taken over the ingrained habit patterns of our lives. It slips in unawares as our attention becomes focused upon the Kingdom of God.

Joy makes us strong. I'll never forget the day I heard the words of Agnes Sanford: "On one of my most joyful and therefore most powerful days. . . ." I do not remember the rest of the statement, but I never forgot the connection she made between joy and power. I have found this to be true, and I imagine you have also. On those days when the joy of the Lord seems to engulf us, there is an almost unhindered flow of God's life and power from us to others.

Celebration is a grace because it comes unmerited from the hand of God. It is also a Discipline because there is work to be done. In Hebrews, we are instructed to "continually offer up a sacrifice of praise to God, that is, the fruit of lips that acknowledge his name" (Heb. 13:15). The sacrifice of praise is the work to which we are called. In the Old Testament, there was a morning and an evening sacrifice. That, I think, is a good beginning for all New Testament

72

priests, of which you are one. Begin the day with the morning sacrifice of praise, "Lord, I love you, adore you, worship you, desire your will and way . . ." Conclude the day with the evening sacrifice of thanksgiving, "Thank you, Lord, thank you for your love, your presence, your strength and grace . . ." And as we do this, the fire will fall upon the sacrifice of our lips just as it did upon the altar of old. God's joy will come, and there will be dance and song and joy unspeakable and full of glory.

Before long, we will find ourselves taking a "thanksgiving" break rather than a coffee break at ten and at two. Soon so rich and full will be our experience that we will desire to be continually in His presence with thanksgiving in our hearts. And all of this will be occurring while we are carrying out the demands of our days—eating, working, playing, even sleeping. Belief in God turns into acquaintanceship and then into friendship. We look into the face of God until we ache with bliss; as Frank Laubach witnessed, "I know what it means to be 'God-intoxicated.' "

As noted before, this joy is beyond the pseudo-gaiety of superficial religion. It is in no way connected with the "smile if you love Jesus" froth of today. It is not even necessarily tied to spiritual ecstasy. Its source is found in the assurance of being rooted and grounded in God. It is the experience known to all the saints and confessed by Brother Lawrence, "Lord, I am yours, dryness does not matter nor affect me!"

Daily Scripture Readings

Sunday: The Lord has triumphed gloriously / Exodus 15:1-2, 20-21.

Monday: The joy of the Lord / 2 Samuel 6:12-19.

Tuesday: Bless the Lord / Psalm 103.

Wednesday: Praise the Lord / Psalm 150.

Thursday: Hosanna! / Luke 19:35-40, John 12:12-19.

Friday: Walking and leaping and praising God / Acts 3:1-10.

Saturday: Hallelujah! / Revelation 19:1-8.

73

Study Questions

1. Do you enjoy God?
2. There is a body of teaching that instructs us to praise God *for* all things; there is another that urges us to praise God *in* all things. Do you feel that the difference between these two bodies of teaching is significant? If so, why?
3. Imagine that some close friends in your church have just received the news that their eight-year-old daughter has been killed in an automobile accident. Should your attitude with them be, "Weep with those who weep"? Or should it be, "Rejoice in the Lord always: again I say, rejoice"?
4. Why do you think a wholesome evening of side-splitting laughter with friends does you so much good?
5. Why do you think human beings often find celebration so difficult?
6. Which do you like better: spontaneous bursts of joy or planned expressions of celebration? Why?
7. If you are in a study group, would you be willing to devise together some hearty holy shout and try it out together before dismissing the meeting?
8. How about planning a family, nonholiday celebration this year?
9. Do you find it easy to laugh at yourself?
10. At the close of this study, what covenant *must* you make with the Lord?

Suggested Books for Further Study

Cornwall, Judson. *Let Us Praise*. Plainfield, N.J.: Logos International, 1973. (A simple, nuts-and-bolts book on the subject of praise in corporate worship.)

Howard, Thomas. *Chance or the Dance?* Wheaton, Ill.: Harold Shaw Publishers, 1969. (An engaging plea for the "old myth" of imagination and a devastating critique of the "new myth" of modern secularism.)

MacDougall, Bruce. *Rejoice in the Lord*. Nashville, Tenn.: Abingdon Press, 1978. (A celebration of all those "unexpected" changes in life that often cause confusion but can bring doxology.)

74

Reid, Clyde. *Celebrate the Contemporary*. San Francisco: Harper & Row, 1972. (A happy book about the author's personal pilgrimage and, particularly, his encounters with the human potential movement.)

Smith, Hannah Whitall. *The Christian's Secret of a Happy Life*. Westwood, N.J.: Revell Company, 1952. (First published in 1870, this work has become a genuine classic on the life of joy.)

Wainwright, Geoffrey. *Doxology: The Praise of God in Worship, Doctrine and Life*. New York: Oxford Press, 1980. (The best modern work on the subject. In 609 pages, Wainwright perceptively discusses Christian faith and life from the viewpoint of praise and worship.)

SCRIPTURE INDEX

OTHER RENOVARÉ RESOURCES FOR SPIRITUAL RENEWAL

Celebrating the Disciplines
by Richard J. Foster and Kathryn A. Yanni

Embracing the Love of God
by James Bryan Smith

Songs for Renewal
by Janet Lindeblad Janzen with Richard J. Foster

Spiritual Classics
co-edited by Richard J. Foster and Emilie Griffin

A Spiritual Formation Journal
created by Jana Rea with Lynda L. Graybeal

A Spiritual Formation Workbook
by James Bryan Smith with Lynda L. Graybeal

Streams of Living Water
by Richard J. Foster

Wilderness Time
by Emilie Griffin

OTHER BOOKS BY RICHARD J. FOSTER

Celebration of Discipline
The Challenge of the Disciplined Life
Freedom of Simplicity
Prayer: Finding the Heart's True Home
Prayers from the Heart
Richard J. Foster's Study Guide for Celebration of Discipline
Seeking the Kingdom